Walking the
Way of the Heart

Practical Lessons for Spiritual Living

G. STEVE KINNARD

Walking the Way of the Heart

Practical Lessons for Spiritual Living

The Way of the Heart
Christian Spiritual Formation Series
Volume Two

Illumination Publishers International
www.ipibooks.com

ipi

Walking the Way of the Heart – Practical Lessons for Spiritual Living
© 2006 by G. Steve Kinnard

09 08 07 06   1 2 3 4 5

ISBN 0-9776954-5-X

Cover and interior layout: Toney C. Mulhollan

Illumination Publishers International
1190 Boylston Street, Newton, Massachusetts 02464
www.ipibooks.com

Contents

Dedication

To my wife of twenty-five years

Leigh Kinnard

Happy 25th Anniversary

For over twenty-five years you
have held my heart captive

and to

our children

Chelsea Danielle Kinnard

and

Daniel Steven Kinnard

You keep our hearts forever young

Acknowledgements

Special thanks to:

My wife, Leigh Kinnard, for her helpful suggestions on the draft. My wife is a deeply spiritual person who connects with God and people on a much deeper relational plane than I do. I valued her input on this book because I knew that if she got something out of reading it, then many other people would be strengthened by it as well. Leigh, thanks for your help on this project and on all my projects.

Toney Mulhollan, my publisher, thanks for encouraging me in my writing.

Dr. Douglas Jacoby, for reading through this material and commenting on it.

Dr. David McAnulty, psychologist and member of the Boston Church of Christ, for mentoring me in my thinking about how to build an emotionally healthy church. I am always grateful for the opportunity to learn from David. Thanks for reading through this text.

Steve Staten, evangelist of the church in Chicago. Thanks for being willing to read through my manuscripts and giving me your reflection on my ideas.

A special note of recognition to my co-worker in the Hudson Valley ministry, Coach Shane Engel. Thanks for covering for me while I was in the Bat Cave finishing this book. I'm glad that God has allowed us to serve in the ministry together. You, your wife Sara, and your children are special to our family.

Additional thanks to:

My family—Leigh, Chelsea and Daniel.

The elders, staff and members of the New York City Church of Christ.

All my close friends in the Hudson Valley Region of the church.

My high school English teacher, Mrs. Hickman, who taught me to love reading. To my college professor, Dr. Porter King, who encouraged my writing.

Sifu Karl Romain who has been a source of great strength and encouragement to me. Sifu Linda Morrissey, Jiao Lian Russell Rosado, Si Hing Jon Edmond and the staff of Romain's Kung Fu for your encouragement.

Introduction

"Once you have begun to walk with God, you need only keep on walking with him and all of life becomes one long stroll—such a marvelous feeling."[1]

–Etty Hillesum, holocaust victim

This is the second in a four volume series on Christian Spiritual Formation. The first volume in this series, *The Way of the Heart*, explored the topic of the heart both biblically and theologically. It laid a foundation for a healthy discussion of what it means to walk the way of the heart.

Toward the beginning of volume one, I tried to set the tone for our discussion by using the metaphor of a journey to describe the choice we have of walking the way of the heart or the way of legalism. I wrote:

> Imagine that you are walking alone through some dense woods on a beautiful spring morning that envelopes you with a crisp air that invigorates and energizes. You begin this journey through these woods to find God. You begin by getting lost. You lose yourself in the forest. You feel nothing of the outside world—no cars, no planes, no music, no human voices—only the rustling leaves of the trees that surround you. Since you don't know where God is, you begin to walk. In walking, you hope to find the path to God. You feel the softness of the earth under your feet as you navigate the rocks and the fallen trees along the floor of the forest.
>
> Your journey is soon halted as you come to two roads in the forest. The roads head in different directions. One is a road that has been well traveled and is easy to spot. The undergrowth of the forest has been worn away by the constant flow of travelers on this road. It seems the easy way. It is clearly marked and not difficult to follow. There is no guesswork in following this road. It is the road that is traveled by most. It is marked with a sign that is freshly painted with bright red lettering on a white background that reads, "The Way of Legalism." Is this the path to God?

The other road is hardly discernible from the thick canopy of the forest. It is obvious that few people have traveled down this road. The encroaching forest has almost obliterated this path. There are remains of a sign, fallen over long ago and overgrown by leaves and brush. You recognize the leaves. A voice rings in your ears. It is the voice of an old friend who taught you long ago, "Leaves of three—let them be." This is poison ivy. You grab a stick and carefully push away the leaves and lift the sign back to its place. The lettering on the sign is difficult to read. It has been worn away by seasons of rain and snow. At first it looks like it reads, "he Way o he ear." But that doesn't make any sense. So you take your hand and rub some dirt off the lettering of the sign, revealing an "H" and then a "t." You see now that the last word is not "ear," but "Heart." You keep rubbing until you you reveal the sign's true message, "The Way of the Heart." You choose to travel the path labeled "The Way of the Heart." Thus you begin your journey toward God.[2]

In the following chapters, we will explore these ideas more deeply. To get the most out of this volume, you should read the first one. If you have not done that, then at the very least, get out your Bible and do a personal Bible study on the heart before you read further.

Walking the Way of the Heart is a collection of practical lessons dealing with the heart. The subtitle, *Practical Lessons on Spiritual Living* describes the purpose of the book. This book is intended to help you make Christianity practical and livable. The first book was a study in Biblical principles (theology and theory). This book is about applying those Biblical principles to our spiritual life. Here we apply the teachings on the heart to our everyday walk with God. That's why it is entitled, *Walking the Way of the Heart.*

Knowledge of God's Word is a wonderful thing. But too often, I've seen people with a great intellectual knowledge of the Word who did not apply the teachings of the Bible to their lives. What is the use of having a head filled with knowledge if that head is disconnected from the heart? Biblical knowledge should translate into spiritual living.

Consider this book your travel companion as you walk down the path marked The Way of the Heart. It is a field manual for your journey. Now that you know what the way of the heart is, you will need help walking down that path. Read the manual. Study it. Talk about it with friends. Write in it. Keep a journal in it. Use it for a few weeks or the next couple of months to help you grow spiritually.

The proposed third volume of the Christian Spiritual Formation Series is entitled, *Living the Way of the Heart.* The subtitle is *Spiritual Disciplines for Spiritual Living.* It is about the classic spiritual disciplines and how they can help us walk the way of the heart. I hope to finish this book within the next year. The proposed fourth volume of the Christian Spiritual Formation Series is entitled, *Maturing in the Way of the Heart.* This book will discuss the Fruit of the Spirit and the Christian Graces. As we mature in the way of the heart, the Fruit of the Spirit and the Christian Graces should become a natural part of our lives. This book will help us to evaluate if the Spirit's fruit and God's grace are growing in our hearts.

I do hope that you benefit from this book. It has been a labor of love for me. It is the book that I always wanted to but never quite got around to writing. I now understand that God was holding me back. He needed to teach me some valuable lessons before I started on this book. I'm sure he'll keep teaching me. Here is what I've learned so far about walking the way of the heart. I hope this book is a blessing to you on your journey as you walk the way of the heart.

—GSK
New City, New York,
2006

Endnotes
1 As quoted in Lewis B. Smedes, *The Art of Forgiving* (New York: Ballantine Books, 1996), 113.
2 G. Steve Kinnard, *The Way of the Heart* (Newton, Mass.: Illumination Publishers International, 2006), 10.

Abba,

Bless us on our journey as we walk the way of the heart.

In the name of Jesus
Amen

Walking the
Way of the Heart

A journey of a thousand miles begins with a single step.
—Chinese Proverb

Spiritual greatness has nothing to do with being greater than others. It has everything to do with being as great as each of us can be.[1]
—Henri J.M. Nouwen, spiritual writer and theologian

Remember the forest that we talked about in the introduction of this book? We came across two roads: the Way of Legalism and the Way of the Heart. We have chosen to walk the Way of the Heart. Along this road there are many valuable lessons that we can learn. As you follow the way of the heart, keep these lessons in mind. They will help you on your journey. They will keep you walking the way of the heart.

Endnotes

[1] Henri J.M. Nouwen, *Can You Drink the Cup?* (Notre Dame: Ave Maria Press, 1996), 83.

Chapter One

The Heart as a Reservoir

The place to improve the world is first in one's own heart and head and then work outward from there.[1]

−From *Zen and the Art of Motorcycle Maintenance*

No Gas, No Go

Have you ever tried to start a car or a lawn mower when it was out of gas? Feels foolish, doesn't it? I remember one sunny, hot, humid afternoon in late August. I worked for an hour on my lawnmower, trying to get it to start. I checked the battery to make sure it was fully charged. I checked the spark plugs to make sure they were firing. I tried starting it with the choke on and with the choke off. As the church song goes, "I tried and tried; I tried and I tried." I tried until I almost cried. I was ready to junk the whole lawnmower and buy a new one. I even asked one of my neighbors to come and take a look at it. He walked over to the lawnmower and asked the most obvious question of all, "Did you check the gas?" That's the one thing I had not done. The lawnmower had no gas. I was trying to get it to run on empty. Internal combustion engines don't run without fuel. I felt more than a little silly trying to get that engine to run without gas. How do you feel when you are trying to run your spiritual life without fuel? Like the internal combustion engine, our spiritual life will not run without gas.

In the hustle and bustle of life, it is easy to forget to refuel our spiritual lives. We have work to do, relationships to build, bills to pay and movies to see. We have to watch our diet, watch our shows and watch our kids. We need to repair the fence, mow the lawn and take out the trash. With all of this, who has time to refuel spiritually? We often are running on empty without even noticing.

Proverbs 4:23 reads, "Keep your heart with all vigilance, for from it flow the springs of life." What is vigilance? It means to keep constant guard over something. If a couple entrusted their newborn baby to you, you would watch that small baby with vigilance. This is how we must look out for our heart.

The Bible says that above all else we must guard our hearts. Our hearts are a treasure. How are we doing taking care of that treasure? We take care of other things in our lives. We feed our stomachs when they growl for food. We brush our teeth at least once a day. Do we take care of the needs of our hearts?

Do we feed our hearts with Scripture? Do we give them the cool waters of meditation? Do we exercise them with prayer?

Store Up What is Good

Bernard of Clairvaux, a spiritual writer, noted:

> If then you are wise, you will show yourself rather as a reservoir than as a canal. A canal spreads abroad as it receives it, but a reservoir waits until it is filled before overflowing, and thus without loss to itself [it shares] its superabundant water.[2]

Are you a canal or a reservoir? A canal channels the flow of water without storing any water away for a later time. Therefore, if the water supply is shut off, the canal will eventually run dry. It has no water to give. A reservoir stores water. The water is there for use now or for use later. When the water supply is shut off, the reservoir holds water, and will continue to hold it.

In Luke 6:43-45 Jesus talks about the treasure we have in our heart. He speaks about doing things out of the abundance of the heart. Jesus says:

> No good tree bears bad fruit, nor does a bad tree bear good fruit. Each tree is recognized by its own fruit. People do not pick figs from thorn bushes, or grapes from briers. The good man brings good things out of the good stored up in his heart, and the evil man brings evil things out of the evil stored up in his heart. For out of the overflow of his heart his mouth speaks.

Our heart is a reservoir. We should be storing good in it. Yet we often treat it as though it were a canal, and we don't focus on storing good in our hearts. Are we taking time to replenish the good in our hearts? Is there an abundance of good stored up in our hearts?

No matter who you are, you have a spiritual side. There is a soul within you that needs to be fed. You have a heart that God has placed within you. Your heart is a reservoir. This is true whether you are a pre-teen, teen, college student, young single, young married, single with kids, married with kids, grandparent or a "golden oldie." You will either feed your heart or let it starve. You will either encourage it or discourage it. You will either nurture it or abuse it. You will store either good in it or evil.

To store good in the heart, we need to make sure that the reservoir of our heart stays in good condition. When I was a pre-teen growing up in Tennessee, I would plant a garden every summer. I planted the garden so that I would have my own vine-ripened tomatoes. There is nothing better than a big, juicy, red tomato right off the vine. Before planting the garden, I would clear the plot of ground with a hoe. (We didn't have a tiller.) If luck struck, my neighbor Jerry Duncan would see me out in the hot sun struggling to break the ground with my hoe, and he would bring his tiller over and till the soil for me. I would plant a few bean plants, a few squash plants, but mostly tomatoes. I noticed that after a week or so, the grass that had been so painstakingly cleared would begin to reappear. If I took the time to pull the grass when it was small, it was a small chore. But if I waited until the grass grew tall and took root—the job became enormous. If I neglected the garden, it would soon be overgrown with grass and weeds.

So it is with our hearts. They need care. If we will give them a little care here and there, we will reap a harvest. But left alone, our hearts will soon be overgrown with weeds. The good in our hearts has to be replenished. How do we replenish the good in our hearts? How do we protect our hearts and keep them safe?

Replenish the Reservoir

In Mark 1:32-38 Jesus takes time to replenish the good in his heart. Mark records:

> That evening after sunset the people brought to Jesus all the sick and demon-possessed. The whole town gathered at the

door, and Jesus healed many who had various diseases. He also drove out many demons, but he would not let the demons speak because they knew who he was.

Very early in the morning, while it was still dark, Jesus got up, left the house and went off to a solitary place, where he prayed. Simon and his companions went to look for him, and when they found him, they exclaimed: "Everyone is looking for you!"

Jesus replied, "Let us go somewhere else—to the nearby villages—so I can preach there also. That is why I have come."

Jesus took time to replenish his heart. He went off by himself to be with the Father. He got up, very early in the morning, at a time when others would not disturb him. He did this to replenish the good in his heart. By doing this he was able to keep giving to people and meet the needs around him. It is okay to withdraw from people in order to get reenergized—in order to be with them once again.

We need to replenish the reservoir of our hearts. We can do this in many ways. One way might work better for you than another. Here are some ways to replenish the reservoir of your heart by storing good in the heart:

- Read a good book.
- Listen to some inspirational music.
- Sit by the fire and relax.
- Get up a little early for some extra time with God.
- Take a walk in the woods—just you and God.
- Take time to catch your breath.
- Take a "power nap."
- Get a cup of coffee with a good friend.
- Go on a trip with someone.
- Visit an art museum and gaze at the wonders of human creation.
- Visit a national park and gawk at the wonders of God's creation.
- Stop whatever you are doing and focus on God's goodness, and thank him for your blessings.

Are you treating your heart like a canal or a reservoir? Are your storing good in the reservoir your heart? By replenishing the reservoir of our hearts, we will be able to let good flow from the abundance of our hearts. Take time to focus on the good around you. Take time to store good in your heart.

We walk in the steps of Jesus—
By making a new friend at work.
By helping someone get his or her groceries in their car at the
supermarket.
By noticing that someone isn't at church and giving him or her
a friendly call to find out why.

We walk in the steps of Jesus—
By loving our children with an unconditional love. By making
them feel like they are the most special children in the world.
By loving our spouses in spite of our differences and
disagreements, and by allowing God to form Christ in us
through our marriages.
By sharing Jesus with someone this week.

We walk in the steps of Jesus—
By laughing with a friend.
By fighting temptation.
By loving the unlovely
    Touching the untouchable
    Caring for those no one cares about
    Giving hope to the hopeless, hapless and helpless
And by taking salvation to all.

This is how we walk in the steps of Jesus.

                                        –GSK, 1978

Abba,

    Fill me with your goodness. Let my heart be a
reservoir that is filled with your goodness. And let me
share that goodness with the world around me.

                                        In Him
                                        Amen

Endnotes

1   Robert M. Pirsig, *Zen and the Art of Motorcycle Maintenance: An Inquiry Into Values* (Los Angeles: Audio Renaissance), Tape 11.

2   Source unknown.

Chapter Two

The Heart of Wonderment: Keeping "Wow" in Our Vocabulary

My Dear Wormwood,

"...Never forget that when we are dealing with any pleasure in its healthy and normal and satisfying form, we are, in a sense, on the Enemy's ground. I know we may have won a soul through pleasure. All the same, it is His invention, not ours. He made the pleasures: all our research so far has not enabled us to produce one...."[1]   Uncle Screwtape

–C.S. Lewis, *The Screwtape Letters*

How Is Your Wow?

What "wows" you? What do you gawk at?

I remember a Ziggy comic strip I saw years ago. Ziggy was looking at the sunrise, with his arms raised up in the air. The caption read, "Go God! Go!" The sunrise made Ziggy go, "Wow!" I have a question for you: What "wows" you?

It is easy to get jaded in this life. Things that were a luxury just fifty years ago, like a television or a telephone, are now a normal part of our home. It is not a question of having a television, but how many televisions do you have. Along with the television you must have a video player, DVD player, some type of game system, cable or satellite reception, and maybe even TiVo. It seems that everyone has a cell phone. You can now walk around and be in touch with people at the push of a button. ("Can you hear me now?") Forty years ago computers were too expensive and way too big to have in our homes. Now computers are common. Once again the question is probably not whether you have a computer, but how many computers do you have? Do you have a laptop or a desktop? What type of software comes with it? We have become jaded.

Look at how quickly technology is advancing today. Ten years ago video cameras were big and bulky. They used VHS tapes. Then the tapes got smaller and the cameras got smaller. Then the cameras became digital. Now you can use your digital video camera to take motion pictures, edit them on your computer, and burn them to DVD. You can even record a video on your phone.

You no longer have to go to a recording studio to record music. You can set up a professional quality studio in your basement using your personal computer. You can make CDs and pass them out to your friends.

In the midst of all this, it is easy to get jaded. We have become hard to impress. I recently went to a war movie that was so incredibly realistic that I felt like I was in the battle with the soldiers (actually actors) on the screen. To get any more realistic they will have to start setting off bombs in the theatre. With all the advances in modern technology, we can begin to lose our sense of wonderment.

Losing our sense of wonderment can happen in any area of life. It can happen in marriage. It can happen in parenting. It can happen with something as wonderful as the season of the year that we call Christmas. As children, Christmas was a magical time. You got to decorate the house with lights. You got to put up a tree inside the house. You got to write letters to a mysterious fat man in a red suit who lived at the North Pole, and you got to ask him for a toy that you wanted. Then on Christmas morning, you got out of bed, looked under the tree, and the toy you had asked for was under the tree. This was magical. It was the wonderful mystery of Christmas. But over time, the mystery fades. It's called growing up.

When we think about God, we need to have a childlike faith. Do you have a sense of wonderment when you think about God? Nothing is bigger, greater, grander, more awesome, more powerful, more extraordinary, more spectacular, more inspiring than God. But if we are not careful, even our wonderment with God can fade.

We must not let our awe of God fade. We must keep our sense of wonderment toward God. When is the last time you thought about God and just said "WOW"? When it comes to God, we must keep "wow" in our vocabulary.

Say "Wow!" to God's Greatness

O Lord, our Lord
     how majestic is your name in
all the earth!

You have set your glory
     above the heavens.
from the lips of children and infants.
     you have ordained praise
because of your enemies,
     to silence the foe and the avenger.

When I consider your heavens,
     the work of your fingers,
the moon and the stars,
     which you have set in place,
     what is man that you are mindful of him?
You made him a little lower than
     the heavenly beings
 and crowned him with glory
     and honor.

You made him ruler over the
     works of your hands;
     you put everything under his feet:
all flocks and herds,
     and the beasts of the field,
the birds of the air
     and the fish of the sea,
 all that swim the paths of the seas.

O Lord, our Lord,
     how majestic is your name in all the earth!

–Psalm 8

Look at how God planned the universe, and you'll see that he is *the Master Architect.*[2]

- The tilt of the earth—at a 23.5 degree angle—produces our seasons. If it were not at that exact angle, vapors from the oceans would move north or south and build continents of ice.
- The moon is 230,000-240,000 miles from the earth. The moon controls our tides. If the moon were 50,000 miles from the earth, the continents would be overrun by water and tides would erode mountains. And there would be equally serious consequences if the moon were too far away from the earth to produce tides.
- If the crust of the earth were just 10 feet thicker—not a mile, not a half-mile, not ten yards, just ten feet thicker—there would be no oxygen and no animal life.
- If the oceans were four feet deeper, they would absorb all oxygen and carbon dioxide, and all plant life would die.
- The earth weighs six sextillion tons. (That's a six followed by 21 zeros). Yet it floats in space in perfect balance. It rotates at more than 1,000 miles per hour or 25,000 miles a day. It travels around the sun 600 million miles every year. This means it travels 1,140 miles per hour.
- The earth is perfectly placed from the sun. A few miles closer and we would all burn up. A few miles farther away and we would all freeze to death. Every square yard of the sun produces the energy of 450 eight-cylinder cars.
- The sun is only one star in the Milky Way galaxy. Hold a dime up at arm's length and look at the sky and the dime blocks you from seeing 15 million stars.

> I will praise you, O Lord, with all
> my heart;
> I will tell of all your wonders.
> I will be glad and rejoice in you;
> I will sing praise to your name,
> O Most High (Psalm 9:1-2).

In Isaiah 40:18-26 Isaiah talks about the foolishness of worshiping idols. Why would you fashion a god with your own hands and then bow down and worship your own creation? Where is the wonderment in that?

We worship the Lord God who fashioned us in his image. He created the world and gave us dominion over it. Take time to look at the glory of God's creation. Stand in awe of God. Gawk in wonderment at the work of his fingers. God deserves our praise, our adoration, our highest compliments and our gawking wonderment.

> The heavens declare the glory of
> God;
> the skies proclaim the work of
> his hands.
> Day after day they pour forth
> speech;
> night after night they display
> knowledge.
> There is no speech or language
> where their voice is not
> heard.
> Their voice goes out into all the
> earth,
> their words to the ends of the
> world.
>
> In the heavens he has pitched a
> tent for the sun,
> which is like a bridegroom
> coming forth from his
> pavilion,
> like a champion rejoicing to
> run his course.
> It rises at one end of the heavens
> and makes its circuit to the
> other;
> nothing is hidden from its
> heat (Psalm 19:1-6).

For This World

O God,

We thank thee for this universe, our great home; for its vastness and its riches, and for the manifoldness of the life which teems upon it and of which we are part. We praise thee for the arching sky and the blessed winds, for the driving clouds and constellations on high. We praise thee for the salt sea and the running water, for the everlasting hills, for the trees, and for the grass under our feet. We thank thee for our senses by which we can see the splendor of the morning, and hear the jubilant songs of love and smell the breath of the springtime. Grant us, we pray thee, a heart wide open to all this joy and beauty, and save our souls from being so steeped in care or so darkened by passion that we pass heedless and unseeing when even the thorn bush by the wayside is aflame with the glory of God.

Enlarge within us the sense of fellowship with all living things, our little brothers, to whom thou hast given this earth as their home in common with us. We remember with shame that in the past we have exercised the high dominion of man with ruthless cruelty, so that the voice of the Earth, which should have gone up to thee in song, has been a groan of travail....

When our use of this world is over and we make room for others, may we not leave anything ravished by our greed or spoiled by our ignorance, but may we hand on our common heritage fairer and sweeter through our use of it, undiminished in fertility and joy, that so our bodies may return in peace to the great mother who nourished them and our spirits may round the circle to a perfect life in Thee."[3]

–Walter Rauschenbusch, social theologian

Dear God,

Guard my heart from becoming jaded. Help me keep "Wow!" in my vocabulary. Give me a heart of wonderment. Allow me to always be dazzled by your greatness and grandeur. I want to be a gawker, who with bright-eyed wonder marvels at your majesty. Give me the heart of wonderment.

In your Son's name
Amen

Endnotes

[1] C.S. Lewis, *The Screwtape Letters* (New York: The Macmillan Company, 1943), 49.

[2] This list was originally published in Brennan Manning's *A Ragamuffin Gospel* (Sisters, Oregon: Multnomah Publishers Inc., 1990), 34-36.

[3] Walter Rauschenbusch, *For God and the People: Prayers of the Social Awakening* (Boston: The Pilgrim Press, 1909), 47-48.

Chapter Three

A Heart for the Saved

A Parable

Sarah's life had revolved around the orphanage. The orphanage was the only world she had ever known. She heard from the other girls that she had been dropped off at the front door of the orphanage when she was only one day old. She was now thirteen. Today was her birthday. She was more excited about this birthday than any other birthday that she had ever celebrated. Today she was leaving the orphanage. A lovely couple who wanted to raise her as their own had adopted her.

Imagine Sarah's horror when she discovered that the couple who adopted her did not want to be her parents, but they wanted to use her around the house to cook and clean. They weren't interested in her as a person. They were only interested in what they could get out of Sarah. They were abusive to her and controlling of her. They didn't want to hear of her insecurities, her weaknesses or her fears. These matters were an inconvenience to them. They had a business to run. And Sarah was now a part of that business. Sarah thought she was signing up to be part of the family. The parents had fooled her. Now she realized they were only interested in what she could provide for them.

Sarah's story is a tragic one. The contrast between the tenderhearted hopes of the girl and the callous opportunism of the parents breaks our hearts. But are our hearts as sensitive as this, when it comes to the people who become a part of the church? Have you ever seen this story played out in the church?

A Reality?

Someone reaches out to Sarah, becomes her friend and invites her out to church. After Sarah's first visit, several people reach out to Sarah and invite her to study the Bible. While Sarah is studying the Bible, these new friends spend hour after hour talking with Sarah, listening to Sarah and encouraging Sarah. Finally, Sarah is ready to be a part of the church. Sarah is so excited to be a part of a family that cares so much for her. Over the past few weeks, people have spent literally dozens of hours with her talking through all of her most intimate secrets. Sarah is baptized.

After her baptism, things change. People are no longer calling Sarah to spend time with her. When she has a problem, she has a difficult time reaching anyone on the phone. She is told that she should get with some girl named Judy, and Judy will help her with her problem. Judy was in the studies with Sarah, but Sarah never connected with Judy. She never felt close to her. They have very little in common. Sarah wants to get with Kimberly. Kimberly is the one who invited her to church in the first place. But Kimberly is too busy studying with the next baptismal candidate. What is Sarah to do? She thought she was becoming a part of a family, but now she realizes that most of the attention that she received was to get her in the baptistry. Where is the help now that she has been baptized? Why aren't all the people who were there to help her get baptized just as excited about helping her to mature in Christ?

Until Christ Is Formed in You

What Sarah experienced has happened too often. People are bombarded with love and relationships before they are baptized, but as soon as they are baptized, the relationships dry up. Where are all the people who were there to help her get baptized? Why are the people who baptized her not there to help her mature in Christ?

We have to develop a heart for the saved. We must realize that our work is not finished when someone is baptized. That is just the beginning. Now comes the hard work. We must work with each person until Christ is formed in him or her. We must care for each person as a family member. We must present him or her mature in Christ. We must have a heart for the saved.

Paul had a heart for the saved. In Galatians 4:19 he writes, "I am in the pain of childbirth until Christ is formed in you." He says this to members of the church. Paul wanted to help those who had been saved to become mature in Christ.

We often talk about having a heart for the lost. We have Bible study groups to reach out to the lost. We have evangelistic campaigns to spread the gospel to the lost world. We sacrifice for world missions so that the world can hear about Jesus. All of these things are good and right. We must have a heart for the lost, as we will see in the next chapter.

But do we have a heart for the saved? Do we have study groups to strengthen disciples? Do we have spiritual formation campaigns to help disciples become mature in Christ? Do we sacrifice to make sure that each disciple reaches his or her fullest potential in the Lord? Are we creating family for those who have been saved?

Working with the lost has a certain glamour about it. You think of pulling someone from the gutter, washing him or her off, and getting him or her on the right track. You think about getting people off of drugs, off the streets and into the church. But keeping the saved saved just doesn't have the same glitzy appeal. Churches keep statistics on how many people they baptize. You hear them say, "We baptized one hundred people this year." After evangelistic campaigns, you hear reports, "We just arrived back from an evangelistic campaign in India, where 234 people made Jesus their Lord." But you don't read church reports about keeping the saved saved. You don't read, "This year 100 people became mature in Christ." You don't hear, "We just got back from a campaign in Ghana, where 286 saved disciples became mature." Keeping the saved saved just doesn't have the same glamour as baptizing the lost.

We have to realize that God loves to see us become more mature. Creating family is vital part of the ministry of the church. In Rick Warren's *The Purpose Driven Life*,[1] he lists five purposes that God has for our lives. Purpose #1 is "You were planned for God's pleasure." Purpose #2 is "You were formed for God's family." It is the purpose of God that we become a vibrant member of his family. This means that as a church we need to create a family environment for our members. It means we need to have a heart for the saved.

In John 15:5, Jesus says, "I am the vine, you are the branches." This image implies relationships. When we become disciples, we become connected to each other. When a branch is dying, we need to care for it and nurse it back to health.

In Romans 12:5, Paul used the image of the body to illustrate how the members of the church have different gifts. He uses the same image in 1 Corinthians 12 to make another point, to say to the members of the church, "Hey, you guys need each other!" We need to take care of each other in the same way that the human body takes care of its members. If one part of the body hurts, the whole body hurts. Sometimes the whole body will shut down in order to repair one part of the body that is hurting. If you hit your finger with a hammer, the whole body responds in pain. Every part of your body focuses on the finger. Your hand that held the hammer grabs the hurting finger as if to give it a hug. You place your finger under your arm to console it. Your eyes cry for your finger. You whole body comes to its aid. The body takes care of its members.

Paul also uses the image of family to speak about the closeness and connectedness of the individual members of the church. Ephesians 2:19 states, "Consequently, you are no longer foreigners and aliens, but fellow citizens with God's people and members of God's household." "Members of God's household" is just another way of saying, "You are in God's family." We are family. You don't give up on members of your family. You fight for them. You encourage them. You strengthen them. You pull for them to succeed. You help them mature. You don't let people walk away from a family without trying to win them back.

To have a heart for the saved means that we will try to help each other get to heaven. It means that we will encourage each other to stay strong in the Lord. It means that we will help each other with our struggles and with our sin. It means that we will create a safe place for people to heal from their wounds. It means that we will help each other to mature in Christ.

All You Need Is Love

It's really all about love. People want to be loved. When they are loved, they feel part of a family. Lennon and McCartney sang:

> All you need is love.
> All you need is love.
> All you need is love.

Love is all you need.[2]

The lyrics aren't complex, but they make a great point. When it comes to building family in the church, love is all you need.

The importance of people feeling connected in their church family cannot be overestimated. Having healthy relationships is an important part of life. Dr. Roberta Gilbert, in her book *Extraordinary Relationships*, writes:

> It would be difficult to overestimate the importance of human relationships. If love does not make the world go around, then surely relationships do. In the world of the personal, the world of work, and the world at large, relationships between people are a critical and decisive force.
>
> In the realm of the purely personal—after food, water and shelter—the quality of relationships most often determines the quality of life. In the workplace, the outcome of enterprises often depends on the quality of relationships between people there. Efficiency, productivity, and creativity are the indicators of whether people can balance tasks and relationships. In the community of nations human relationships start and stop wars.[3]

And so Jesus says to his apprentices, "A new command I give you: love one another. As I have loved you, so you must love one another. By this all men will know that you are my disciples, if you love one another" (John 13:24-25). Loving each other is not just a nice principle, not just a good thing to do, not just a sensible precept, it is a direct command of Jesus.

To bring the saved to maturity we need to create an environment where people can grow. We need to make love real. How do we do this? How do we have a heart for one another and love one another? We can begin by practicing the one-another scriptures. These scriptures are there to help us with our relationships. For example, consider these one-another scriptures from the book of Romans:

- 12:10—Be devoted to one another in brotherly love. Honor one another above yourselves.
- 12:16—Live in harmony with one another.
- 13:8—Let no debt remain outstanding except the continuing debt to love one another.

- 14:13—Therefore let us stop passing judgment on one another. Instead, make up your mind not to put any stumbling block or obstacle in your brother's way.
- 15:7—Accept one another, then, just as Christ accepted you, in order to bring praise to God.
- 15:14—I myself am convinced, my brothers, that you yourselves are full of goodness, complete in knowledge and competent to instruct one another.
- 16:16—Greet one another with a holy kiss.

By practicing these and many more one-another scriptures, we can begin to actualize love in our church. We can build family. This will not be a perfect church. There are no perfect churches. If there were, as soon as you or I placed membership at that perfect church—*blam!*—it would no longer be perfect. Churches are often messy places, just as families are often messy. But that is okay, because the church is God's messy place. It is a place where God will transform us. It is place where God will mature us. It is a place where God will help us get to heaven. And it is a place where God will give us a heart for the saved.

Abba,

Create in me a heart for the saved. Help me to see that when someone is baptized, the work for his or her spiritual well-being has just begun. Help me to build family in the church. Help me to practice the one-another scriptures and to walk the one-another way.

In Jesus' name
Amen

Endnotes

1   See Rick Warren's *The Purpose Driven Life* (Grand Rapids: Zondervan, 2002).
2   John Lennon and Paul McCartney, "All You Need Is Love," from *Magical Mystery Tour* (London: EMI Records Ltd., 1967).
3   Roberta M. Gilbert, *Extraordinary Relationships: A New Way of Thinking About Human Interactions* (Minneapolis: Chronimed Publishing, 1992), 3.

Chapter Four

A Heart for the Lost

"Evangelism" is a scary word even to many Christians. I have often heard people who are dedicated members of a church say, "I hate evangelism" or "I don't believe in it," or, usually from the shy, more introverted members of the a congregation, "I'll do anything else for this church, but don't ask me to serve on the evangelism committee."[1]

–Kathleen Norris, spiritual writer

Then there are the "seriously" crushed ones: The flunk-outs and drop-outs. The broke and the broken. The drug heads and divorced. The HIV-positive and herpes-ridden. The brain-damaged, the incurably ill. The barren and the pregnant too-many-times or at the wrong time. The overemployed, the underemployed, the unemployed. The unemployable. The swindled, the shoved aside, the replaced. The parents with children living on the street, the children with parents not dying in the "rest" home. The lonely, the incompetent, the stupid. The emotionally starved or emotionally dead. And on and on and on. Is it true? That is precisely the gospel of heaven's availability that comes to us through the Beatitudes. And you don't have to wait until you're dead. Jesus offers to all such people as these the present blessedness of the present kingdom—regardless of circumstances. The condition of life sought for by human beings through the ages is attained in the quietly transforming friendship of Jesus.

–Dallas Willard, spiritual writer and theologian

In the first volume, I wrote about the heart of the Trinity. In investigating the heart of GOD, we saw that GOD's heart is such that he wants us to grow as people. He wants us to become mature in Christ. GOD wants to form Christ in us. In doing so, GOD allows us to go through tough times. GOD allows us to go through difficult, painful and even hurtful events. Of course, GOD went there before us, blazing a path for us to follow. Jesus endured the pain of the cross as an example for us to walk in his steps. GOD was behind the cross of Jesus, and he is behind our crosses.

With that said, we don't need to forget that Satan has a role to play in evil and suffering. Satan will try to twist our pain to turn us against GOD.

From God or from Satan?

God permits or causes all the painful events we experience as people or as a church, and he can use these events to discipline us. When we become arrogant or legalistic, or when we, as a church, are on the way to becoming a human institution, he has a way of initiating events to stop us in our tracks. Or he may allow us to become a human institution and wallow in mediocrity. When we elevate man to a position higher than God desires, God might discipline us so that we can understand our mistake. Or he may allow us to suffer under the authoritarian oppression of an egomaniac.

As God disciplines us, Satan steps in to take full advantage of the pain we are feeling, in hopes of twisting us against God. He might lead us to lose faith or to distrust people and leadership. And if we allow ourselves to become distracted, we might forget all about our mission, forget the world is lost and in desperate need of God. We could lose our heart for the lost.

Meanwhile, Satan laughs and enjoys our struggle. Satan laughs a despicable, hideous laugh. His demons join him in this laughter. He laughs to mock GOD. He laughs to mock the church. He laughs to mock you and me. Can you hear his laughter?

Listen for his laughter. See how he tries to exploit events to turn brother against brother and sister against sister. See how he tries to get us to forget that we were bought with the blood of Jesus. See how he strips away our unity and promotes suspicion. And hear his laughter.

Seeing What Is

Another way that Satan can take advantage of our struggles is by getting us to focus on our problems so much that we fail to see the lostness of the world around us. Do you see the lostness of the world? Do you understand how dark the darkness is? And do you realize that billions of people are trapped in that darkness? Ephesians 6:12 reads, "Our struggle is not against flesh and blood, but against the rulers, against the authorities, against the powers of this dark world and against spiritual forces of evil in the heavenly realms." We are at war against the powers of this dark world. Can you feel the darkness? Do you sense the lostness of the world? Look at these examples of the world's darkness:

- Recently, the Supreme Court considered ruling to take the phrase "one nation, under God" out of the U.S. Pledge of Allegiance.
- In many of our schools, "God talk" is not allowed. Students are not allowed to read their Bibles, pray, or have Bible discussions during school hours. Where it is allowed, students are often mocked or laughed at for engaging in such activities. At some of these same schools, gay and lesbian clubs are sponsored by faculty members and meet during school hours.

Consider:
- 67% of the victims of sexual abuse are children.
- 34% of those children are under the age of 12.
- Every nine seconds a women is assaulted or beaten.
- Every day, four women die from injuries sustained in a beating.
- Every day, one child dies from injuries sustained in a beating.
- The number one cause of injury in America is not accidental injury. It is physical abuse.
- Over the last five years more women died of physical abuse than all U.S. losses in the Vietnam War.
- 50% of the homeless today are women and children.
- Three times more money is spent on sheltering animals than on sheltering women.
- There are 3.3 million teen alcoholics in our nation.
- Almost 30,000 Americans committed suicide in the year 2000.
- More people die from suicide than from homicide.

- Suicide is the eleventh leading cause of death for Americans. It is the third leading cause of death in young people age 15-24.
- Every year more than 1,000 teenagers attempt suicide.
- There are about 3 suicide attempts per day.
- Right now almost 19 million Americans are clinically depressed.
- Almost 10% of the American population is depressed.
- 35 million suffer depression that warrants treatment. This is 16% of the American population.
- Nearly 20 million Americans suffer from chronic nervousness, panic attacks or phobias.[2]

Can you see the darkness? Can you feel the lostness of the world? Do you have a heart for the lost?

While the world is lost in utter darkness, Satan laughs.

Satan laughs:

While he tempts another person to give up his or her faith and leave the church.

While he tempts one more man to click onto a pornographic web site that will begin a lifelong addiction to pornography.

While he gets one more father to risk the family's financial security by betting on this year's "sure thing."

While he tempts another teenager to get drunk so that he will fit in with the crowd.

While he gets yet another teenager to take ten more pills because this will stop her pain.

While he tempts one more man to walk out on his wife of twenty years because being married is no longer satisfying.

While he tempts another desperate housewife to drown her sadness in alcohol and pills.

While all this happens, Satan laughs. He laughs because we as a church have grown numb to the lostness of the world. Has his last opponent, God's church, closed its doors and called it a day? As he beats up on the world, is no one there to answer his challenge?

Take Heart and Deliver the News

Do you realize there are some things that Satan cannot do? Satan can't push you off a cliff, but he can make jumping look pretty appealing. Satan can't force you to cheat on your wife, but he can persuade you that it won't matter if you do. Satan can't destroy the church. In Matthew 16:18, Jesus says, "On this rock [the rock of Peter's confession that Jesus is the Christ, the Son of God] I [Jesus] will build my church, and the gates of Hades will not overcome it." Satan can't destroy the church, but we can hand it to him. We hand it to him by laying down our Bibles and not caring any more. Apathy or indifference is Satan's greatest weapon.

The mission of Jesus is very clear. "For the Son of Man came to seek and to save what was lost" (Luke 19:10). Jesus felt the lostness of the world. He came to do something about the suffering of the world. He had then and he has still a heart for the lost.

The mission of the church is very clear. Consider these verses:

He (Jesus) said to them, "Go into all the world and preach the good news to all creation. Whoever believes and is baptized will be saved, but whoever does not believe will be condemned" (Mark 16:15-16).

Jesus came and spoke to them saying, "All authority has been given me in heaven and on earth. Therefore Go! Go make disciples of all nations! Baptize them by the authority of the Father, and the Son, and the Holy Spirit! Then teach them to obey all things that I have commanded you! Look, I am with you always to the end of age"[3] (Matthew 28:18-20).

How, then can they call on the one they have not believed in? And how can they believe in the one of whom they have not heard? And how can they hear without someone preaching to them? And how can they preach unless they are sent? As it is written, "How beautiful are the feet of those who bring good news!" But not all the Israelites accepted the good news. For Isaiah says, "Lord, who has believed our message?" Consequently, faith comes from hearing the message, and the message is heard through the word of Christ (Romans 10:14–17).

The mission of Jesus has now become our mission. He left his mission in the hands of the church. Do you feel the darkness? Can you hear the cries of the world? Can you hear the laughter of Satan?

Terry Wardle, in his excellent book, *The Transforming Path*, questions:

> I often wonder why Christ left the responsibility of communicating the good news to people. Surely He knew that there was a real potential that the job would not be done. Regardless, the hope of many rests with the willingness of the few.... Lost and broken people need to hear the message of salvation and Christians are to do the communicating.[4]

Wardle then mentions several reasons why Christians may not share their faith:
- You may not love the world.
- You may not realize that it is your responsibility.
- You may have been put off by the evangelistic methods that you've seen employed by churches in the past.

Wardle writes:

> The best means of sharing the faith are relational. There is no better way to attract a person to Christ than by becoming a true friend to him or her. Sharing common interest builds deep bonds between people. Genuine caring is always the best bridge for Christ to cross between two people. Opportunities to talk about the good news will arise naturally, and broken people will have an honest chance to respond to the gift of life in Christ.[5]

- You may believe people will be put off if you share with them.
- You may believe that you cannot accurately share the gospel with people. Wardle writes:

> Christians can be very effective talking to others by sharing a simple testimony that identifies four things: what life was like before they came to Christ, how they came to know they needed Christ, what they did to accept Christ and how life has changed since they received Christ.[6]

One last question. Where would you be right now if someone had not shared the gospel with you? It may have been your mother or your grandfather; it may have been a school friend or complete stranger; but unless you picked up the Bible and came to faith on your own, someone shared with you and helped you become a Christian. We have all benefited because someone loved us enough to share with us. We now need to reawaken our hearts and share with other people. We need to have a heart for the lost.

Abba Father,

Create in me a heart for the lost. Help me to see how desperately people are hurting without Jesus in their lives. Help me to see their lostness. Help me to remember what it was like to be trapped in the pit of darkness. Help me to speak up. Help me to embrace the mission of Jesus. Help me to embrace the mission of your church. Help me to quiet the laughter of Satan and to give opportunity for the angels to rejoice by inviting one of your children to step from the darkness into the light of the kingdom of your Beloved Son.

In the Beloved's name
Amen

Endnotes
[1] Kathleen Norris, *Amazing Grace: A Vocabulary of Faith* (New York: Riverhead Books, 1998), 300.
[2] Source unknown.
[3] Author's translation.
[4] Terry Wardle, *The Transforming Path: A Christ-Centered Approach to Spiritual Formation* (Siloam Springs, Arkansas: Leafwood Publishers, 2003), 108-109.
[5] Ibid, 110.
[6] Ibid.

Chapter Five
A Heart for the Wounded

> On the last day, Jesus will look us over not for medals, diplomas or honors; but for scars.[1]
>
> —Brennan Manning, spiritual writer

The Healing Elm
—GSK, August 3, 1983

Trees are a wonderful, spectacular part of God's creation. They provide shade in the summer, barriers against the cold winds of winter and beauty all year round. In the spring they provide vibrant colors as they flower, and in the autumn the colors are just as wonderful as the leaves die and drop from the trees. Those leaves that drop provide nutrients that enrich the soil. Trees provide fuel for fire, wood for furniture and houses, and material to make paper. Trees are a glorious part of God's creation.

> He (the righteous) is like a tree planted by streams of water, that yields its fruit in season, and its leaf does not wither (Psalm 1:3).

When I was a kid I loved climbing trees. Every now and then, you can still find me up in a tree. In our backyard we have a tree that is perfect for climbing. When we bought our house, one of the first things that I did was to go into the backyard and climb that tree. I wanted to make sure that it would hold the kids. But I also just wanted to climb it. I have often found my son in the branches of this tree. This tree is special to him. It will always be his friend.

In Jerusalem, my daughter had a special tree in the Garden of Gethsemane. Gethsemane means "olive press," and the trees that grow there are olive trees. The trees in the Garden of Gethsemane aren't suited for climbing high to the heavens, but they have strong, thick branches that hang low to the ground and are great for stretching out on and taking a nap (like a leopard in the African plains). My daughter would stretch out on one particular branch of one special tree in the Garden of Gethsemane. She would lie there and pray or think or clear her mind. This tree was special to her. It will always be her friend.

My wife, Leigh, shared with me that she had a weeping willow tree in her backyard in Henderson, North Carolina when she was growing up. Since it was a weeping willow, she thought that it would be a good place to go when she was sad. She would take her dogs with her under that tree, and they would all have a good cry together. She would water the weeping willow with her tears. This tree was special to her. It was her friend.

When I grew up, we had a Chinese elm tree in our backyard. It was tall and thick and perfect for climbing. My brothers and I would climb to the top of her branches and try to shake each other out. We would catch June bugs on her leaves and tie a string to their legs and fly them around our heads like airplanes. I used to lounge in the shade of this tree and sit on her roots. We became good friends. That tree and I spent countless hours together in the summer. That tree was special to me. We were friends.

After I went away to college, I came home one summer to find my friend dying. Sap was leaking out of her and her leaves were turning brown. Some tree disease was getting the best of her. I asked my dad if anything could be done for her, but she seemed to be beyond help. I went back to school.

On my next trip back home from college, I found my old friend had been cut down to a five-foot stump. There was a huge, barren spot in my backyard where this tree had once stood graceful and tall. The limbs that I climbed as a boy were gone. All that was left was a stump. A tree that once towered over thirty feet in the air, I could now look eye to eye with. I mourned. This tree—a symbol of my youth—was now gone.

But then I went away again. I graduated from college. I went to Mobile, Alabama to teach English at a high school there. The next time I returned home, I found a surprise. The stump of our elm tree, the tree that we had left for dead, was now sprouting new life from its stump. It was growing again. It had been sick and it had been wounded, but it was not dead. It was still alive inside.

That elm became a symbol for me. Just because something looks dead and beyond repair, doesn't mean that its life is over. Perhaps, just below the surface, life still flows. Perhaps healing can still occur. That's why I call my old friend, the healing elm. She is a symbol that no matter how desperate our spiritual lives become, healing can still occur. We are never so dead that we cannot sprout new life. We are wounded, but we still have life in us.

I hope I never give up on a person the way we gave up on that elm. I need to have a heart for the wounded. God has a heart for the wounded. See what God says in Isaiah 56:3-5:

> Let not any eunuch complain,
>   "I am only a dry tree."
> For this is what the Lord says:
>
> "To the eunuchs who keep my Sabbaths,
>   who choose what pleases me
> and hold fast to my covenant—
>   to them I will give within my
> Temple and its walls
>   a memorial and a name
> better than sons and daughters;
>   I will give them an everlasting name
> that will not be cut off."

For the eunuch, his lineage stopped with him. His name ended with his death. This was a very important concept to Old Testament people. In the ancient mind, your name was to live on in your children. Remember the promise to Abraham in Genesis 12 that his descendants would be as numerous as the sand on the seashore or as the stars in the heavens. Remember how important genealogies were in Old Testament times.

The eunuch would never have that. He would have no descendants. His genealogy stopped with him. But God says to the eunuch, "Don't call yourself a dead tree." He tells him that his name would live on. His lineage would not end with him, because God would give him an everlasting name. God would write his name in the sand. God would write his name in the stars for all eternity.

God Has A Heart For the Wounded

God loves the wounded. He never gives up on them. He doesn't leave them to die. He understands wounds. Why does God have a heart for the wounded?

Because Jesus Was Wounded for Us

In the Fourth Suffering Servant Song, Isaiah writes of the wounded Messiah, saying:

> But he was pierced for our
>   transgressions,
> he was crushed for our iniquities;
> the punishment that brought us
>   peace was upon him,
> and by his wounds we are
>   healed (Isaiah 53:5).

God has a heart for the wounded because his own son was wounded to heal our wounds. If God allowed his Son to take upon himself our wounds, then he must have a heart for the wounded.

Hebrews 5:8-9 speaks of Jesus, saying, "Although he was a son, he learned obedience from what he suffered and, once made perfect, he became the source of eternal salvation for all who obey him and was designated by God to be high priest in the order of Melchizedek." When Jesus took on human form, he learned obedience the same way all of us learn obedience—through our suffering. Jesus knew what it was like to suffer. He can relate to us in every way. He knows wounds. And through Jesus, God has a full understanding of what it means to be wounded. God has a heart for the wounded.

It is important to note that we shouldn't look at all wounds as bad. Wounds teach us lessons. You can look at your scars and tell the story of how you got that scar. Our spiritual scars are there for a reason—to teach us a spiritual lesson. We learn obedience through suffering.

Because God is the Giver of Wounds and the Healer of Wounds

God has a heart for the wounded. But with that being said, we also need to realize that, at times, God gives us wounds to teach us lessons.[2] Speaking to the people of Jerusalem, God said, "I will devastate this city and make it an object of scorn; all who pass by will be appalled and will scoff because of its wounds" (Jeremiah 19: 8). God was going to discipline his people. He was going to wound them so that they would learn a lesson.

But God would also heal their wounds. As soon as the lesson was learned, God would be there as doctor and nurse to heal the wounds that he had given them. Jeremiah 30:17 reads:

> "But I will restore you to health and heal your wounds,"
> declares the Lord, "because you are called an outcast, Zion for
> whom no one cares."

God is the giver of wounds, but he is also the healer of wounds. Both of these ideas come together in a single verse in Hosea 6:1-2, where Hosea prophesies to the people of Israel, saying:

> "Come, let us return to the Lord.
> He has torn us to pieces,
>   but he will heal us;
>   he has injured us
> but he will bind up our wounds.
> After two days he will revive us;
>   on the third day he will restore us,
>   that we may live in his presence."

In this verse, we clearly see that God wounds us, but he also heals our wounds. Our wounds can be a lesson from God. When they are, then he will heal them when they are ready to be healed.

We don't like to be wounded. When we are wounded, we want to ease the hurt and take away the pain. But if our wound comes from God, we need to feel the pain and learn from the hurt. We need to see what God is trying to teach us. In his time, he will heal our wounds. Trust him. He has a heart for the wounded. He will heal your wounds in his time.

Because God Heals Us Through Jesus' Wounds

How does God heal our wounds? He heals them through the wounds of Jesus. In 1 Peter 2:23-24, the apostle writes, "He himself bore our sins in his body on the tree, so that we might die to sins and live for righteousness; by his wounds you have been healed. For you were like sheep going astray, but now you have returned to the Shepherd and Overseer of your souls." Jesus died on the cross to heal our wounds. Not just the wounds of the best and the brightest, but all of our wounds.

God has a heart for all of the wounded: the diseased, the broken, the tired, the down-and-out, the loser, the underdog, the poor, the hungry, the convict, the felon, the addict, the sinner, the less-than-perfect, the beggar, the orphan, the widow, the fatherless, the stepchild, the quirky, the nerdy, the goofy, the geeky, the needy, the pitiful, the imbalanced and the unbalanced, the abnormal, the diseased, the deformed, the dysfunctional and the maladjusted.

God has a heart for those of us will never be all-state, all-American, all-world or all-universe. He has a heart for those of us who will never be superstars. He has a heart for those of us who will never have our names written in lights. He will give us "an everlasting name." He loves the poor as much as the rich, the sick as much as the healthy, the losers as much as the winners, the third world as much as the first world, the have-nots as much as the haves, the introverts as much as the extroverts. God is ready to give them all "an everlasting name."

Being with the Wounded

Did you ever see the movie *Gone With The Wind*? It's a classic. When I was in the eleventh grade, my English teacher, Mrs. Hickman, asked me if I had ever seen *Gone With The Wind*. I had to tell her, "No, Mrs. Hickman, I've never seen that movie." I'll never forget her response. She knew that I wanted to be a preacher, so she responded, "Mr. Kinnard, you'll never get through the pearly gates without seeing *Gone With The Wind*." Since Mrs. Hickman was right about most everything, I made a point to see the movie. After seeing the movie, I thought to myself, "Perhaps Mrs. Hickman was right after all. A boy from Tennessee needed to see *Gone With the Wind*."

In the movie, just before the break for the intermission, there is a breathtaking scene in which Scarlett O'Hara walks through a plaza in Atlanta to attend to confederate soldiers injured in battle. As Scarlett begins to walk among these injured soldiers, the camera pans back to show more and more wounded Confederates. After a few seconds, the camera has swept back so far that you can see the entire plaza. All you can see is a sea of wounded soldiers. You get the sense that the whole of humanity was wounded in the war.

That scene reminds me of the church. The church is a sea of wounded humanity. We are all the casualties of war. We have been wounded by pride, hatred, prejudice, lust, broken homes, broken marriages, broken dreams, rape, incest, infighting, backstabbing, gossip, lies, addictions, selfishness, life and the world. Satan has wounded us. Sin has wounded us. We have, at times, wounded each other.

In the midst of all these wounds, we need to develop a heart for the wounded. Poor Scarlett O'Hara! As she travels through this sea of wounded humanity, she is lost. She doesn't have a clue as to what she should do. She has a confused look on her face. Nothing has prepared her for what she sees. She wants to run. She wants to hide. She wants to get away. But how can you run from so much pain? The wounded are everywhere.

At times we are like Scarlett. The wounds of the lost are too much to bear. How can you face so much heartache in the world? Just this week I heard of a young boy who was sexually molested by an older man. What do you say to that boy? What do you say to his parents? Just this week I spoke with a woman whose brother was brutally murdered. What do you say to that woman?

Often there is nothing to say. What do you say to an incest victim? What do you say to someone with borderline personality disorder? What do you say to someone who was raped over and over by a lecherous uncle? What do you say to a family who just lost everything they owned in a fire? What do you say to the fireman who received burns on more than 70% of his body while attempting to put out the fire? What do you say to a child who just lost his mom and dad in a plane crash?

Instead of trying to say something, just "*be*." Just be there in the moment. Just be there in the present. The wounded want us to be with them.

When we make the decision to just be, then we are offering the person hope. We offer them hope through relationship. We are letting them know: "I can't understand your pain, I don't know how badly you are hurting, I don't know what to say to you, and I don't know what to do for you; but I am here for you." By being present with them in the moment, you are offering them the most precious item you have to offer—yourself.

Jesus is Gonna Fix It

Being there for hurting people is often a frightening proposition. If we enter into their suffering, won't we suffer with them? Yes, we will. Henri J. M. Nouwen writes, "No one can help anyone without becoming involved, without entering with his whole person into the painful situation, without taking the risk of becoming hurt, wounded or even destroyed in the process."[3] It is scary being there for people. But it is through sharing their suffering that we can help with their suffering.

Sharing their suffering is different than trying to "fix" their pain. We have the fix-it syndrome. We want to make everything better. We want to heal people's wounds right away. We want to fix people. We want to say just the right thing. We want to quote just the right verse. We want to fix it.

It's not our place to fix anything. One of my favorite church songs is "Jesus—He Will Fix It."[4] After every mention of trouble, the words go, "My Jesus, he will fix it, my Jesus he will fix it, my Jesus he will fix it in a while." It's Jesus' work to fix it. God heals wounds. We need to trust God to fix it. And in his good time, he will.

Knowing that God is the healer of wounds, takes the pressure off us. Now we don't have to fix it. We don't have to say the perfect thing. We don't have to do exactly want is needed. God will do the talking and the doing so that we can just be. We can be with the person in the moment.

I'm part of the walking wounded. When my wounds hurt deeply, I don't need anyone to say anything to me. I just need someone to be. To be there with me in the hurt. To be there with me in moment. To be there until I find the strength to move on.

We are all wounded. None of us is perfect. I don't even know how to define "normal" any more. I recently heard this joke:

> During a visit to the mental asylum, a visitor asked the Director what criterion was used to define whether or not a patient should be institutionalized.
>
> "Well," said the Director, "we fill up a bathtub, then we offer a teaspoon, a teacup and a bucket to the patient and ask him or her to empty the bathtub."
>
> "Oh, I understand," said the visitor. "A normal person would use the bucket because it's bigger than then spoon or the teacup."
>
> "No." said the Director, "A normal person would pull the plug. Do you want a bed near the window?"

We are all wounded. We all have our quirks. We shouldn't feel that we have to fix each other. None of us has the expertise to do that. Our Jesus, he will fix it. Let's care for one another. Let's love one another. Let's empathize with one another. Let's encourage one another.

God has a heart for the wounded. He wants to give them an everlasting name. The church is a sea of wounded humanity. Let's be there for each other in the moment.

Abba,

I hurt. My wounds ache. But in my hurt, help me to remember that you hurt because of my hurt. Help my hurt to remind me of the hurt around me. Help me to have a heart for the wounded.

In the name of him who was wounded for us all
Amen

Endnotes

1 Brennan Manning, *Ruthless Trust* (San Francisco: Harper San Francisco, 2000), 48.

2 Some are uncomfortable with the idea that God gives wounds. They want to place all the blame for wounds on Satan and sin. But it is difficult to get around a verse that says, "He (God) has injured us" (Hosea 6:1). Some would rather say that God allows others (including Satan) to injure us. This chapter is not an answer for the problem of evil or the problem of pain. In all honesty, I have yet to find a totally adequate answer for those questions. I live with the ambiguity that a totally Sovereign and perfectly loving God causes (or at the very least allows) great suffering and pain to occur in our lives. This is called *trust* (1 Peter 2:23). The point of this chapter is that I don't need to have an answer for the problem of pain; I just need to *be* there with people as they suffer through their pain.

3 Henri J. M. Nouwen, *The Wounded Healer* (New York: Image Books, Doubleday, 1972), 72.

4 "Jesus—He Will Fix It." Words: Traditional, Music: Traditional.

Chapter Six

The Trusting Heart

The splendor of a human heart which trusts that it is loved gives God more pleasure than Westminster Cathedral, the Sistine Chapel, Beethoven's Ninth Symphony, Van Gogh's *Sunflowers*, the sight of ten thousand butterflies in flight or the scent of a million orchids in bloom.[1]

—Brennan Manning, spiritual writer

Peace of Mind produces right value, right value produces right thought, right thought produces right action, right action produces right work, which will be a natural reflection for others to see of the serenity at the center of it all.[2]

—From *Zen and the Art of Motorcycle Maintenance*

When you've got nothing, you've got nothing to lose.[3]

—Bob Dylan, singer poet

Surrender and Trust

I originally entitled this chapter "The Surrendered Heart." I hear the word "surrender" used often in the church. We talk about surrendering our lives to God. We talk about the power of a surrendered life. We talk about surrendering control of our lives to Jesus. We talk about surrendering our rights in becoming disciples. "Surrender" is a good word. There is nothing wrong with the word "surrender."

But then I read Brennan Manning's excellent book, *Ruthless Trust*, and I decided to change the name of the chapter to "The Trusting Heart." *Ruthless Trust* is a powerful book, and I highly recommend it to everyone. As I read it, I realized that although I often hear about surrender, I don't often hear about trust.

Why do we readily talk about surrender, but speak less often of trust? I'm not exactly certain why. I've not done a survey on the subject. But, I do have a hypothesis. I believe that we have unconsciously accepted a belief that surrender is active and trust is passive. When this happens, we will chose active over passive any day of the week.

I believe that we look upon surrender as something we control. Surrender is our decision. We choose to surrender. We make up our minds that it is time to cut our losses and surrender. Think of the phrase, "I surrender my right to _____." This puts the emphasis on you. You can't frame that statement using the word "trust." Trust puts the emphasis on the other party.

In addition, surrender seems more heroic than trust. Surrender is more of a military term. And we love military terminology. In war, you could keep on fighting, but you choose to surrender. Again the emphasis is on you. You forget that you just got beat in battle. No, I could keep on fighting, but I'll surrender instead. And after we surrender, in the back of our minds we say, "I could have won if I had just kept on fighting." So we tend to think of surrender as an active choice that we have control over.

Trust is a different matter. Trust seems more passive. With trust the ball is in the other person's court. When you trust someone, he has the power. There is nothing heroic about that. To trust is to admit your helplessness. To trust is to admit that you are powerless. You trust in someone else's heroism. When you trust someone, you are saying, "I completely and utterly believe that you have my best interests at heart. Please take absolute control of my life." This is trust.

Also, when we speak of surrender we usually speak of surrendering some *thing* in our lives, but when we speak of trust we usually talk about trusting some *one*. Trust is a more relational term. We don't usually trust inanimate things.[4] You don't trust a television. You might trust or distrust a television commentator. We trust people. That is why trust is such a great word to use in connection with God. By saying we trust God, it implies that we have a relationship with him. Trust is relational.

Consider these verses from the Psalms:

- Trust in the Lord and do good; dwell in the land and enjoy safe pasture (37:3).
- He put a new song in my mouth, a hymn of praise to our God. Many will see and fear and put their trust in the Lord. Blessed is man who makes the Lord his trust, who does not look to the proud, to those who turn aside to false gods (40:3-4).
- When I am afraid, I will trust in you. In God, whose word I praise, in God I trust; I will not be afraid. What can mortal man do to me? (56:3-4)
- I will say of the Lord, "He is my refuge and my fortress, my God, in whom I trust" (91:2).
- Those who trust in the Lord are like Mount Zion, which cannot be shaken but endures forever (125:1).
- Let the morning bring me word of your unfailing love, for I have put my trust in you. Show me the way I should go, for to you I lift up my soul (143:8).

To trust we have to become children. We have to forget that we are adults and that we have all these years of experience and that we know so much and that we are so smart and that we are so educated and that we have done so much and seen so much and been through so much. To trust means that we have to follow. We have to admit that someone else knows more than us; we have to admit that we don't have everything figured out; we have to admit that we don't know it all; we have to admit that someone else might know more than we do. Trust implies a loss of control. Trust implies that you will let someone else take control. Trust is difficult. It's simply too hard to do.

My reasoning could be off here. But there must be some reason why we prefer the word "surrender" to the word "trust." At the end of the day, both are good words. But for this chapter of this book, the subtle nuances of the word "trust" work better.

As apprentices of Jesus, we must have trusting hearts. Yes, we must surrender to Jesus. Yes, we must deny self and take up our cross and follow him. But we also must learn to trust him. And I believe that after surrender and after self-denial comes that last and most difficult step of all—trust.

What is Trust?

One of my favorite old hymns is "Trust and Obey." I like the melody, but I love the words.

> When we walk with the Lord in the light of his Word,
> What a glory he sheds on our way!
> While we do his good will, He abides with us still,
> And with all who will trust and obey.
> Trust and obey
> For there's no other way
> To be happy in Jesus
> But to trust and obey.
>
> But we never can prove the delights of his love,
> Until all on the altar we lay;
> For the favor He shows, and the joy He bestows,
> Are for those who will trust and obey.
> Trust and obey
> For there's no other way
> To be happy in Jesus
> But to trust and obey.[5]

One of the most challenging things that anyone could say to us is, "Just trust me." What is your inclination when someone says, "Just trust me on this one"? We don't like to trust. Why? Because we have been "burned" so many times in life. I've been betrayed before, and I'm sure that you have as well. I've had people who acted as though they were my friends. They told me, "If you ever need me, I'll be there for you." But then a day arrived when I did need them. In my darkest hour, I turned to them for help. I didn't ask them for money or for a huge sacrifice. All I wanted was a little empathy during a time of real pain. But they betrayed me. They wronged me. They turned their backs on me. After this happens, it is difficult to trust.

For a self-acknowledged people-pleaser like me, it is even more devastating when you are betrayed. When you have spent enormous amounts of energy trying to get someone to like you, betrayal hurts deeply. It is a terrible hit on your self-esteem and feelings of self-worth. It makes you want to put up barriers all around you that say, "I will not trust again."

Brennan Manning is most famous for his book *The Ragamuffin Gospel*. But I prefer his book *Ruthless Trust*. In this book Manning defines trust:

> Faith arises from the personal experience of Jesus as Lord.
> Hope is reliance on the promise of Jesus, accompanied by the expectation of fulfillment.
> Trust is the winsome wedding of faith and hope.[6]

He summarizes this thought with the formula:

> "Faith + Hope = Trust"[7]

Trust is built on faith and hope. Manning writes, "Faith and hope work together to form a trusting disciple."[8]

Faith in the Personal Experience of Jesus as Lord

When we hear the words, "Just trust me," we get cynical and skeptical. We put up our guard, especially if someone has ever wronged us. Tell someone who has been abused most of his or her life to "just trust." That's like telling a giraffe to become a cricket. How can you "just trust" when you have no "trust" left in you?

But that is exactly what Jesus says to us. He says, "Just trust me." John 14:1 reads, "Trust in God; trust also in me." Of course, Jesus works with us so that we can faithfully put our trust in him. He is willing to let us start out with "baby steps." He'll say to us, "Just try trusting in this situation and see how it turns out for you." He doesn't expect us to run a marathon the first time we tie on a pair of running shoes. But he will coach us and get us ready to run the marathon. Over time, we learn to place our complete trust in Jesus.

We trust Jesus because we have experienced his love. We trust him because we have personal knowledge of him. We have first hand knowledge of his faithfulness. We trust him in small ways, and he comes through. So we up the ante. We trust him in larger matters, and he still comes through. He proves that he is trustworthy. We trust him because we have learned through experience that he won't fail us.

Brennan Manning tells the story of a family enjoying a summer vacation at a lake. The family had three children ranging from four to twelve years of age. One day the father was outside doing work, the mother was in the kitchen cooking up the next meal, and the children were in the yard enjoying the warmth of the sun. The youngest child, a four-year-old boy named Billie, decided to wander off to the lakefront to look at the aluminum boat glistening in the sunlight. He walked to the end of the boat dock where he lost his footing and went splashing into the water.

His twelve-year-old brother heard the splash and immediately began to yell for his father. His father came running to the dock and jumped into the murky water to look for Billie. But the lake was eight feet deep and the father had to come up for air twice before he finally spotted Billie at the bottom of the lake. Billie had his arms wrapped around a pier and was holding onto the pier with all his might. His father went down one last time, pried Billie's hands off the wooden pier, and carried him to safety on the dock.

When the commotion of the event finally died down, the father asked Billie, "What were you doing down there holding onto the pier?" The boy replied, "Just waiting on you, Dad. I was just waiting on you."[9]

That is trust based on experience.

Expecting the Fulfillment of Jesus' Promises

> Christianity is mainly wishful thinking. Even the part about Judgment and Hell reflects the wish that somewhere the score is being kept.
>
> Dreams are wishful thinking. Children playing at being grown-up are wishful thinking. Interplanetary travel is wishful thinking.
>
> Sometimes wishing is the wings the truth comes true on.
> Sometimes the truth is what sets us wishing for it.[10]
>
> –Frederick Buechner, spiritual writer

> He who has a *why* to live for can bear with almost any how."[11]
>
> –Friedrich Nietzsche, German philosopher

We trust in Jesus as a person, but we also trust his promises. For my father's generation a person's personal guarantee meant something. You could seal a deal with a handshake. That is the way business was done. But today in the United States, no one in his or

her right mind would seal any type of serious business deal with
only a handshake. A handshake and a team of attorneys would be
adequate, but a promise isn't good enough anymore.

But you can still trust the promises of Jesus. His word is his
bond. He won't renege on a promise. I love Paul's statement in 2
Corinthians 1:20, "For no matter how many promises God has
made, they are 'Yes' in Christ. And so through him the 'Amen' is
spoken by us to the glory of God." We say "Amen" (which means "so
be it") through Jesus, who always keeps his promises.

I love the old church song entitled, "Standing on the Promises."
It goes:

> Standing on the promises of Christ my King,
> Through eternal ages let His praises ring;
> "Glory in the highest!" I will shout and sing,
> Standing on the promises of God.
>
> Standing on the promises that cannot fail,
> When the howling storms of doubt and fear assail,
> By the living word of God I shall prevail,
> Standing on the promises of God.
>
> Standing on the promises of Christ the Lord,
> Bound to Him eternally by love's strong cord,
> Overcoming daily with the Spirit's sword,
> Standing on the promises of God.
>
> Standing on the promises, I cannot fall,
> List'ning every moment to the Spirit's call,
> Resting in my Savior as my all in all,
> Standing on the promises of God.
>
> Standing on the promises, standing on the promises,
> Standing on the promises of God, my Savior;
> Standing on the promises, standing on the promises,
> I'm standing on the promises of God.[12]

And what are the promises of Jesus? They are glorious.
Hebrews 8:6 states, "But the ministry Jesus has received is as superior
to theirs as the covenant of which he is mediator is superior to the
old one, and it is founded on better promises." Peter talks about

Jesus' promises being great and precious in 2 Peter 1:4, by writing, "Through these he has given us his very great and precious promises, so that through them you may participate in the divine nature and escape the corruption in the world caused by evil desires."

The promises of Jesus are beyond our wildest dreams or expectations. They include:

- Salvation
- A home in heaven
- His steadfast love
- The Holy Spirit as our strength
- Christ's return
- Life to the full
- Eternal life
- Forgiveness of sins
- A room in God's mansion

But the promises of Jesus are mostly for the hereafter and not the here-and-now. This flies in the face of one of today's most popular theological ideologies, prosperity theology. I can't stand prosperity theology. It misleads people. Prosperity theology teaches that if you trust God, he will give you all your wishes in the here-and-now. God will take away your disease. He will pay all your bills and get you out of debt. He will straighten out your kids and make them respectful, obedient, all-world student-athletes with musical and artistic talent. God will cause everything that you touch to turn to gold. Sounds nice. Only one problem: God never promised you a rose garden. Prosperity theology is unbiblical.

I do believe that the Christian life is the best life to be lived in the here-and-now. You may well ask, "Why is that?" Because it is the only life with hope. And hope makes life qualitatively better. Hope keeps us going.

Without hope, the days are dark and dreary, the sun doesn't shine, your body aches, your bones hurt, your smile fades to a frown, laughter turns to mourning,

As the guys on the old television comedy show *Hee-Haw* use to sing:

> Gloom, Despair and agony on me
> Deep, dark, depression. Excessive misery.
> If it weren't for bad luck.

I'd have no luck at all.
Gloom, Despair and agony on me.[13]

Victor Frankl was a psychiatrist. After surviving the Nazi death camps, he wrote a memoir of his experiences and developed a psychological treatment called logotherapy. After reflecting on his time in the camps, Frankl noted that the difference between the people who were able to survive the atrocities of the death camps versus those who did not survive was attributable to the fact that those who survived continued to search for meaning in their suffering. They still had hope in a future. Frankl writes, "The prisoner who had lost faith in the future—his future—was doomed. With his loss of belief in the future, he also lost his spiritual hold; he let himself decline and became subject to mental and physical decay."[14]

Frankl tells the story of one prisoner who had a dream in mid-February 1945 that the camp would be liberated on March thirtieth. As March thirtieth approached, it became clear that the camp would not be liberated by that day. The man lost hope. On March twenty-ninth the man became sick, on March thirtieth he lost consciousness and on March thirty-first he died.

Frankl contrasts this to two people who clung to life because they believed that someone or something was waiting for them in the future. One believed that his child was safe in a foreign country, and she awaited his release. The other was a scientist who needed to finish a series of books that he had started. People who had a hope for the future kept fighting. But when people had no hope for the future, they stopped fighting for survival. Frankl writes, "Any attempt to restore a man's inner strength in the camp had first to succeed in showing him some future goal."[15]

Hope gives us a future. When you trust in hope, you fight. Hope is powerful. Jesus gives us hope. Hope for the here and now, but greater hope for the hereafter. Let's trust in hope. Let's trust in his promises.

Trust Does Not Mean Things Will Work Out as We Planned

One promise of Jesus is, "In the world you will have trouble" (John 16:33). Hello, televangelists and prosperity preachers! What do you do with this verse? Life isn't meant to be heaven on earth.

Heaven comes after this life. In the here and now, we have Trouble. And yes, that's with a capital "T."

Trust does not mean that everything in life will work out the way we plan on it working out. It doesn't mean that we will not feel pain. It doesn't mean that we not ever hurt again. Trust is most genuine when we trust while we are in the throes of hurt and pain. Job said, "Even though He slay me, yet will I trust Him" (Job 13:15 KJV).

I am an obsessive guy by nature. I am prone to addictions. If I start reading the first word of a book, then I feel that I must complete that book before I begin a new one. Trusting God doesn't mean that he will take away my obsessive compulsions. But he will help me adjust to life as an obsessive-compulsive person. He can even teach me how to help other people that struggle in this area.

I tend to be a melancholy person. My moods are more down than up. I've never been diagnosed as being clinically depressed, but that may be because I've never gone in for a diagnosis. I've read enough about depression to know that it is a struggle of mine. I don't expect God to take away the struggle. But I know that he will give me strength to survive the battle. And in the meanwhile, he will teach me valuable lessons about myself so that I can help other people.

There are times when I get stressed out and anxious. Even as I've been working on this book, I've had to stop several times and quiet my anxious spirit. I've had to practice deep breathing exercises to help me relieve my stress. I study Tai Chi because it helps harmonize my body and mind and makes me less stressful. I don't expect God to take away all the stress in my life. That's what heaven is about. But in the meanwhile, as I'm waiting in the here and now for the hereafter, God helps me through. He strengthens me. And all the while, a little more of Christ is being formed in me. That, to me, is trust. Trust is knowing that even as you are walking through the darkest moments of your life that God is still there walking with you, and he is forming Christ in your heart.

I find the words of Philip Yancey helpful here. In his book, *Rumors of Another World*, he writes:

> Trust does not eliminate the bad things that may happen, whatever sparked our fear in the first place. Trust simply finds a new outlet for anxiety and a new grounding for confidence:

God. Let God worry about the worrisome details of life, most of which are out of my control anyway. "Do not be anxious about anything, but in everything, by prayer and petition, with thanksgiving, present your requests to God," Paul wrote. "And the peace of God, which transcends all understanding, will guard your hearts and minds in Christ Jesus."

When I question the practicality of those words in view of all the terrible things that have happened to Jesus' followers over the years, I remind myself that Paul wrote them from a Roman prison cell. God's peace indeed "transcends all understanding."[16]

Dearest Abba,

I entrust myself to you every moment of every day. I place all my hope in you. I give you my fears, my anxieties, my doubts and my frustrations. Help me to realize that even when it seems that you are absent, that you are in those times the most present. Those are the times that you are working in your own mysterious way to form Christ in me.

Through Jesus
Amen

Endnotes

1 Manning, *Ruthless Trust*, 2.

2 Pirsig, Tape 5, Track 3.

3 Bob Dylan, "Like a Rolling Stone," from *Highway 61 Revisited* (New York: Columbia Records/CBS, 1965), side 1, track 1.

4 Of course it is possible to trust in wealth (gold and silver) or in power (bows and chariots) or in false gods (Asherah poles and statues of Baal). But we generally speak of trust in connection with another person.

5 "Trust and Obey," words by John H. Sammis and music by Daniel B. Towner, 1877.

6 Manning, *Ruthless Trust*, 86.

7 Ibid.

8 Ibid.

9 A story told by Dennis Rainey, related in Manning's *Ruthless Trust*, 95-96.

10 Buechner, *Wishful Thinking: A Theological ABC* (New York: Harper and Row, Publishers, 1973), 96.

11 As quoted in Victor Frankl's, *Man's Search For Meaning* (New York: Pocket Books, 1959), 95.

12 "Standing on the Promises," Words and music by R. Kelso Carter. Published in 1886.

13 As remembered from my childhood.

14 Frankl, 95.

15 Ibid, 97.

16 Yancey, *Rumors of Another World* (Grand Rapids: Zondervan, 2003), 218.

Chapter Seven
The Heart of a Student

Who teaches you? Whose disciple are you? Honestly.

One thing is sure: You are somebody's disciple. You learned how to live from somebody else. There are no exceptions to this rule, for human beings are just the kind of creatures that have to learn and keep learning from others how to live. Aristotle remarked that we owe more to our teachers that to our parents, for though our parents gave us life, our teachers taught us the good life.[1]

–Dallas Willard, spiritual writer and theologian

The word "disciple" is found all over the New Testament. It is also widely used across churches today. It is used so often that it has lost much of its meaning. Instead of using the word "disciple," each time you see the word "disciple" in the New Testament, substitute the word "student" or "apprentice." Are you an apprentice of Jesus? Are you a student of Jesus? Is he your rabbi/teacher? We are to be students of Jesus. But what does it mean to be a student of Jesus?

Jesus Is Our Teacher

To be a student of Jesus means that Jesus is our teacher/rabbi. Every student needs a good teacher. During my school years, it wasn't until the eleventh grade that I began to enjoy literature class. That year Mrs. Hickman was my teacher. She taught me to love literature. Because of Mrs. Hickman, I continued my study of literature in college. While in college, I met Dr. Porter King. He taught me love of writing. Because of him, I worked on my writing skills to the point of becoming an author. Good teachers changed my life. That is what good teachers do. Jesus was and is a good teacher.

Throughout the gospels, Jesus is described as being a teacher. Even other teachers, the scribes, recognized Jesus as a teacher. Matthew 8:19 records, "Then a teacher of the law (a scribe) came to him and said, 'Teacher, I will follow you where you go.'" This is an example of a teacher (the scribe) coming to the Master Teacher, Jesus, and saying, "I want to be your student." Although the scribe did not follow through with his pledge, he recognized that Jesus was the Master Teacher. This is where our relationship with Jesus must begin and where it must end. We are always students studying at the feet of Jesus.

Jesus had a teacher/student relationship with his closest followers. Matthew 9:11 reads, "When the Pharisees saw this, they asked his disciples, 'Why does your teacher eat with the tax collectors and sinners?'" The Pharisees perceived that the disciples of Jesus were his students. Jesus taught them as a Rabbi teaches students or as a Master teaches an apprentice. Jesus told his disciples in Matthew 11:29, "Take my yoke upon you and learn from me." In Mark 13:28, Jesus said to them, "Now learn this lesson from the fig tree." Jesus taught his disciples as a Rabbi. He had a teacher/student relationship with them.

Jesus saw himself as a teacher. In John 13:13-16 Jesus says, "You call me 'Teacher' and 'Lord,' and rightly so, for that is what I am. Now that I, your Lord and Teacher, have washed your feet, you also should wash one another's feet. I have set you an example that you should do as I have done for you." Jesus acknowledged to his disciples that he was their teacher and their master (Lord). He also told them that he taught not only through spoken lessons but also by the power of his example.

Jesus is our teacher. He is the best teacher that we could ever have. We must live our lives in a student to teacher relationship with him. Good teachers change lives. If we will live in a student to teacher relationship with Jesus, then he will change our lives.

Be a Good Student

Even the best teacher can only take a student as far as he is willing to learn. We have the greatest teacher in human history—Jesus. There is no question about that. But if we were to sift through the annals of human history, where would you rate as a student?

Over the past several years, I've had the great privilege of teaching at the Hope School in Patterson, New Jersey on Saturday mornings. The Hope Schools were started several years ago to offer students in rough urban areas an opportunity to attend great extra-curricular classes after school during the week and on weekends. I've taught classes in creative writing, drums and the martial arts. I've enjoyed helping out in these classes. In my time there, I've noticed that there are several types of students. Here are a few:

The "What Am I Doing Here on a Saturday Morning?" Student

It's pretty easy to tell which students want to be in your class and which don't. I remember one student who did a disappearing act in my class. I saw him sitting in his chair. Then I turned to write something on the board. When I turned back around, he wasn't in his chair any longer. I had no idea where he was. I looked all over the room. Finally, I found him twisted up in one of the lockers in the back of the room like a contortionist. If carnival tricks are ever offered at the Hope School, then he'll be number one in the class. But on most Saturday mornings, he wasn't too keen on being in a creative writing class.

The "You're Not My Daddy and I Don't Have to Listen to You" Student

These are the kids who challenge your authority. They want to be at the school, but they also want to be in control of the class. They think they know better than you. Somehow in their ten to twelve years of life they've been able to accumulate more knowledge and more life experience than you have in your thirty to forty years on the earth.

I had one student who challenged me at every turn. He thought he was slick as butter on a hot skillet. He had a comeback for everything I said. So I had to have a talk with him. I let him know that I was the teacher, and he was the student. I let him know that I wasn't going to allow him to disrespect me in my class. I didn't talk down to him, but I didn't talk to him as a peer, either. I let him know the difference between the teacher and the student. We got along fine after that talk. An ordering of the relationship was needed. He needed to be the student, and I needed to be his teacher.

The "I'm Interested but I Don't Want My Friends to Know It" Student

These are the students who try to be "too cool for school." They aren't really there to make trouble. In fact, they are grateful to be at school. But they don't want you or anyone else to know that they are glad to be there. So they affect disinterest. Every now and then they make snide comments about the class. In creative writing class, they will write stories about severed body parts or about bowel movements. They do this to get a chuckle out of their classmates. Overall, they are harmless. They want to be liked. They want you to teach them, but they want you to use the side door instead of the front door. The front door works better, but if the student only offers the side door, then that is what the teacher must walk through.

The "I'm Interested and I Don't Care Who Knows It" Student

These are the students who are there to learn anything and everything they can. At the Hope School, I teach drums with Dr. Marcus Williams. We had one student who was too young to sign up for our drum class, but he showed up at the beginning of every drum class banging on the drums. Each week I would have to escort him to his assigned class. Then there was a two-week stretch when Dr. Williams and I both had to miss class because of our travel schedules. When we returned, we discovered that this young student had sat through the previous two classes and learned the drum parts that we had been rehearsing. He had caught up with the class in two weeks time. We were so impressed with his desire to learn that we allowed him to stay in the class for the rest of the term. He became one of our best students.

Of these four types of students, most teachers prefer the fourth type, but they would settle for the third type. Good teachers don't give up on the first two types of students, but they have to work on them and get them to want to be in the class and to want to learn. They have to reach their hearts.

But in all fairness, learning depends on the student as much as the teacher. Some students don't want to learn. When I was in college, I sat in a class with a friend from my hometown. He did not want to be in school. He was there because his father made him attend class. He was failing every subject. One beautiful spring day, we sat beside a huge window that sat very close to the ground outside. I saw my friend gazing out that window during the class. He never once looked at the teacher. With about ten minutes left in class, he stood up and announced to the class, "I'm outta here!" Then he stepped through the window and never returned. He left his books sitting on his desk. I never saw him again. He didn't want to be a student. Some people don't want to be students.

In Matthew 13:3-9, Jesus describes four types of soils—the pathway soil, the rocky soil, the thorny soil and the good soil. The parable of the soils is not about literal soil; it is about hearts. You could say it is about being a student, because Jesus is talking about how receptive a heart is to his word. After telling the parable, Jesus explains it to his disciples.

The pathway soil represents people who do not embrace the message of Jesus. Satan snatches the message from their hearts.

The rocky soil stands for the persons who love the message, but don't take it deep into their hearts and make changes based on the message. When tough times come, they abandon the message.

The thorny soil represents people who receive the message and start living by it. But thorns begin to choke them. They are concerned with the worries of life and the deceitfulness of wealth. The message loses its effectiveness. They are unfruitful because of the distractions of life.

The good soil stands for people who receive the message and live by it. By hearing, retaining and persevering, they produce an abundant crop—some one hundred, some sixty, some thirty times what was sown.

The parable drives us to a question, "What type of soil am I?" Everyone fits into one of these categories. Jesus wants us to be good soil. He wants us to have hearts that are willing to learn from him.

Jesus is the Master Teacher, but what type of student are you? Do you ask Jesus to teach you the lessons you need to learn? Are you eager to see things in your character that need to change? Are you a student of the word of Jesus? What type of student are you?

How Do We Learn from Jesus?

Students learn in different ways. Some students are fine sitting at a desk in a classroom listening to a lecture. For other students, this is torture. They need interactive lessons that stimulate their senses. Schools are beginning to realize that students don't all learn in the same way. Schools need to develop different approaches to meet the needs of their students. Jesus, as a Master Teacher, teaches us in many different ways. Here are some of the avenues that Jesus uses to teach his students.

Experience

> Knowing the heart of Jesus and loving him are the same thing. The knowledge of Jesus' heart is a knowledge of the heart. And when we live in the world with that knowledge, we cannot do other than bring healing, reconciliation, new life, and hope wherever we go.[2]
> –Henri J.M. Nouwen, spiritual writer and theologian

You've probably heard that there is no teacher like experience. Jesus teaches us through the lessons we learn in life. Some of these life lessons are difficult to learn. But we need to pay attention to our life lessons, or we will be destined to keep repeating them. Peter writes to students of Jesus who were undergoing intense persecution, saying:

> Though now for a little while you may have had to suffer grief in all kinds of trials. These have come so that your faith—of greater worth than gold, which perishes even though refined by fire—may be proved genuine and may result in praise, glory and honor when Jesus Christ is revealed (1 Peter 1:6b-7).

In February of 2003, the church where I minister underwent a tremendous change. At first, I wasn't a very good student of those changes. I wanted to protest against everything that God was trying to teach me. Then I prayed, "Okay, God, show me exactly what you want me to learn from all of this." I began to see God's hand in the events. This book on the heart is the product of the lessons that God wanted me to learn.

What I went through in the spring of 2003 was painful. It wasn't nearly as painful as what happened to me in the fall of 2003. Through a sickness in my family and through sickness in my own emotional health, God taught me how to persevere through intense pain. I experienced deep, intense, emotional pain. I've lived with this pain ever since. I've experienced bouts of depression, anxiety attacks and, at times, have despaired of life itself. I've experienced intense, paralyzing emotion pain. I once faced it on a daily basis. Now it is better.

Through all of this I see that God is refining me. I can empathize and sympathize with others like never before. In his book *Exquisite Agony*, Gene Edwards says that most people recognize that they have to bear the cross of Jesus. But Edwards makes the point that before Jesus went to the cross, he also had to go through the Garden of Gethsemane. Edwards says that we must all experience our Gethsemane before the cross. Gethsemane is agony. But we learn valuable lessons from our Gethsemane.

The Word

In John 8:31-32, Jesus says to his disciples, "If you dwell in my word, you are my genuine apprentices. And you will know the truth, and the truth will liberate you."[3] To be a true apprentice of Jesus, we must dwell in his word. Dwelling in the word gives us freedom. It liberates us from sin, from self-righteous religion and from our own inner turmoil. To be free in Jesus is to be free indeed.

I have been a preacher for over twenty-five years. In that time there is at least one thing that I have learned—people who become disciples of Jesus love his Word. Just recently I've seen the power of the Word operate in three people's lives. One was a woman with grown children who came to church looking for completeness. She devoured the Bible and found that a relationship with Jesus was the answer. Another was a teenage girl who had suffered many setbacks in her life. She started reading the Bible just to see if it could help. She read the Scriptures voraciously. In doing so she learned about Jesus, fell in love with Jesus and gave her life to him. The third was a Jewish man who had never read the New Testament. He wondered what was different about Jesus. I encouraged him to read the Sermon on the Mount. After he read it once, he said, "I get it. I see what was different about Jesus." He fell in love with Jesus and gave his life to him. Like the others, this man digested large quantities of the Word of God. All three of these people feasted on God's Word, and the Word fed their spirits.

If you feed yourself a steady diet of the Word of God, your spiritual life grows. Fall in love with God's Word. Let it speak to your spirit. Dwell upon the word of God.

The Holy Spirit

In John 16:12-15, Jesus tells his apprentices:

> I have much more to say to you, more than you can now bear. But when he, the Spirit of truth, comes, he will guide you into all truth. He will not speak on his own; he will speak only what he hears, and he will tell you what is yet to come. He will bring glory to me by taking from what is mine and making it known to you. All that belongs to the Father is mine. That is why I said the Spirit will take from what is mine and make it known to you.

The Holy Spirit will teach us about Jesus. He will work in our lives to form Christ in us.

The Holy Spirit takes what is Jesus' and makes it known to us. He helps us see the world differently. He makes us people with vision. He turns us into dreamers. In the movie, *Butch Cassidy and the Sundance Kid*,[4] Paul Newman plays Butch Cassidy and Robert Redford plays the Sundance Kid. At one point in the movie they have this conversation:

> Sundance: *What's your idea this time?*
> Butch: *Bolivia.*
> Sundance: *What's Bolivia?*
> Butch: *Bolivia. That's a country, stupid! In Central or South America, one or the other.*
> Sundance: *Why don't we just go to Mexico instead?*
> Butch: *'Cause all they got in Mexico is sweat and there's too much of that here. Look, if we'd been in business during the California Gold Rush, where would we have gone? California–right?*
> Sundance: *Right.*
> Butch: *So when I say Bolivia, you just think California. You wouldn't believe what they're finding in the ground down there. They're just fallin' into it. Silver mines, gold mines, tin mines, payrolls so heavy we'd strain ourselves stealin' 'em.*
> Sundance: (chuckling) *You just keep thinkin', Butch. That's what you're good at.*
> Butch: *Boy, I got vision, and the rest of the world wears bifocals.*

Sundance says, "Butch, you're thinking!" And without missing a beat, Butch shoots back "Yes, I'm a man of vision and the rest of the world is wearing bifocals." What about you? Are you a person of vision or are you wearing bifocals? The Holy Spirit will give you vision.

Other People

In the Great Commission Jesus instructs his apprentices to "Go into all the world and make disciples of all nations, baptizing them in the name of the Father, and the Son and the Holy Spirit" (Matthew 28:18-20). But after people are baptized, the work of the teacher isn't finished. Jesus goes on to say, "And teach them to obey." The teacher needs to teach the newborn disciple how to obey. How do we learn about Jesus? We learn through other people who teach us how to mature as we follow Jesus.

More mature disciples are to share their experience in the walk of discipleship with less experienced disciples. But this also means that less experienced disciples need to seek out more experienced disciples and ask to be taught. We need to be students of other people.

But notice that Jesus is describing a teacher/student relationship. He is using a mentor/learner model. He is not talking about a lord/servant relationship. He is not speaking of an over/under discipleship model. How someone teaches a student to obey is just as important as what someone teaches. We teach not just with our words, but also in how we model the relationship.

As an apprentice of Jesus, find a few people you admire and easily relate to and ask them to teach you to obey Jesus. Study their spiritual life. Study their walk with God. Walk with them on the journey. I call this self-initiated discipleship or self-imposed training. You are not being assigned to another person as though you were his or her project; you are asking someone to help you become mature in Christ. It is important to have the right people in your life. When you make a decision of who you want to be your spiritual mentor, you need to own the decision. We all need spiritual mentors. But we need to choose for ourselves who those mentors are going to be.

Larry Crabb writes, "Three things keep me from cynically giving up on the hope of finding life-changing reality in Christ: Scripture, the Holy Spirit, and a few people."[5] We need people in our lives. I know that I need people in my life. I am grateful to people who have taught me how to be a better disciple. I am grateful for the people who modeled Jesus to me. They have enriched my spiritual life. They have been a blessing to me.

Dearest Father,

Help me to have a student heart. Help me to be a learner. Please teach me your ways so that I can walk in them. Instruct me through my experiences, through your Word, through your Holy Spirit and through your people. Help me to always learn the exact lesson that you are teaching. And as I'm learning, form Christ in my heart.

Through Jesus
Amen

Endnotes

[1] Willard, 272.

[2] Henri J.M. Nouwen, *In the Name of Jesus* (New York: Crossroads, 1992), 41.

[3] Author's translation.

[4] *Butch Cassidy and the Sundance Kid*, a film. Produced by John Foreman. Directed by George Roy Hill. Written by William Goldman, 1969.

[5] Larry Crabb, *Inside Out* (Colorado Springs: NavPress, 1988), 219.

Chapter Eight

A Grateful Heart

Let's say I interviewed ten people, asking each the same question—"Do you trust God?"—and each answered, "Yes, I trust God," but nine of the ten actually did *not* trust him. How would I find out which one of the ragamuffins was telling the truth?

I would videotape each of the ten lives for a month and then, after watching the videos, pass judgment using this criterion: the person with an abiding spirit of gratitude is the one who trusts God.

The foremost quality of a trusting disciple is gratefulness. Gratitude arises from the lived perception, evaluation, and acceptance of all life as grace—as an undeserved and unearned gift from the Father's hand.[1]

–Brennan Manning, spiritual writer

Gratitude
GSK
March 16, 1999

Each day we are given hundreds of opportunities to thank
God for the splendor of life.
Do we seize or squander the opportunities?

When we rise from bed, sit to eat, brush our teeth, clean our glasses,
kiss our children, pet the dog, start the car, pop the lid on the Dr. Pepper can,
turn on the TV, turn off the TV, grab a snack, make a call, buy our
groceries, wash our socks, run on the treadmill, gasp for air, brush our
hair, fight through traffic, go to work,
drink a cup of coffee, run an errand, speak with a friend, read the paper,

smell the roses,
fold the underwear, surf the 'Net, listen to music, eat some chocolate,
bask in the sun, walk on grass,
sing, leap, jump or run.

Every single day, hundreds of reasons to say thanks.

God gives us every opportunity that we have in life—big or small, important or trivial, purposeful or purposeless. Every good and perfect gift comes from God. He has breathed into our nostrils the breath of life. He has given us the death of his Son. He has given us his Spirit, his kingdom, his Word, his love, his grace, his mercy, his compassion, his all. What are we giving back?

What does God want back? He wants our all. He wants our heart. But he wants us to have a grateful heart. A heart of gratitude. A heart that says, "Thank you." This is what we can give back to God.

To Become a Grateful Person

A Grateful Heart Begins with Appreciating God

We must understand that everything that we enjoy in life comes from God. James 1:16-17 reads, "Don't be deceived, my dear brothers. Every good and perfect gift is from above, coming down from the Father of heavenly lights, who does not change like shifting shadows." Every good and perfect gift comes from God. Your very life is a gift of God. We must begin here. We must acknowledge that everything that we enjoy, everything that we cherish, even life itself is a gift. And it is a gift perfectly chosen just for us.

When someone does something nice for us, how do we respond? We usually respond by saying, "Thank you." Or perhaps we will take the time to write a nice note. We might even decide to do something nice for them in response.

What if someone did something huge for you? What if somebody donated bone marrow so that you could have a bone marrow transplant? What if he gave you one of his kidneys? What is someone donated his or her heart to you—I mean a literal heart—

how would you respond? Dr. Lombard, a neurologist in Rockland County, New York, recently gave me a book entitled, *The Grateful Heart: Diary of a Heart Transplant.*[2] (Thank you, Dr. Lombard, for the book.) The book tells the story of Candace Moose, who after receiving immunizations to go on a medical missionary trip to Malawi for the relief of AIDS victims, fell prey to a rare and often fatal disease called Giant Cell Myocarditis. Candace tells in her own words about the heart transplant that she received and the medical care that was given to her. The book is her thank-you note to the heart donor and to the medical staff that nursed her back to health.

But it is also a very moving appeal for everyone to consider being an organ donor. Moose writes, "Right now, today, no fewer than 85,000 Americans await a lifesaving transplant. Eight thousand of those live in the New York area. Tens of thousands more need tissue transplants. A new name is added to the national waiting list every thirteen minutes. A single donor can save up to eight lives through organ donation—and improve the quality of life of dozens of others through corneal, bone, skin and other tissue transplants. Seventeen men, women and children of all races and ethnic backgrounds die every single day for lack of a donated organ. Yet tragically, nationwide, half of the families asked about donation do not consent. Why? Mainly because they are unaware of their loved one's wishes, or they have misinformation about organ donation itself, or the critical need for this gift."[3]

Moose was so grateful for her new heart that she had to say "Thanks." She did so by writing a book that appeals to all of us to become organ donors. When someone does something nice for us, it should be a natural response to say "Thank you."

What if someone cured you of leprosy? How would you respond to that? Luke tells the story of ten lepers who were cured by Jesus (Luke 17:11-19). Ten were cured, but only one came back to Jesus to say, "Thanks." The question that comes from this story is, "Are you like the nine, or are you the one who returned to say 'Thanks'?" We need to have grateful hearts. Grateful hearts take the time and make the effort to say, "Thanks." And we need to begin by saying, "Thanks," to God for giving us life and giving us the ability to appreciate the good things in life. A grateful heart begins here.

Make a List of All the Things for Which You Are Thankful

Oh God, I thank thee
for all the creatures thou has made,
so perfect in their kind—great animals like the elephant and the
rhinoceros,
humorous animals like the camel and the monkey,
friendly ones like the dog and the cat,
working ones like the horse and the ox,
timid ones like the squirrel and the rabbit,
majestic ones like the lion and the tiger,
for birds with their songs.
O Lord give us such love for thy creation,
That love may cast out fear,
And all thy creatures see in man
Their priest and friend,
Through Jesus Christ our Lord.[4]

—George Appleton,
general editor of *The Oxford Book of Prayer*

When I was growing up, I learned a song in Sunday school
that goes:

Count your many blessings
Name them one by one
Count your many blessing
See what God has done.[5]

We need to stop and count our blessings. This gets us in touch
with the many wonderful gifts God has given to us. It also helps us to
realize how wonderful life is.

Think of the hundreds of nice things that you enjoy in life.
Make a short list right now of ten or fifteen things that you truly
love: a friendly smile, a beautiful day, the color orange, Taylor guitars,
college football, a hamburger from the grill, the laughter of children,
a comfortable couch, the sound of a Harley, the smell of perfume, a
Christmas bonus, a good book, a romantic date, a perfect sunset, a
starry night, a full moon, puppies, dinner at a nice restaurant, family
vacation. God gives us all these nice things.

Now take a moment and thank God for every single blessing
on your list. Take time here and there to add to your list. See how

long your list becomes. Make this your "Thanksgiving List." You might keep the list in your personal organizer or write it in the back of your Bible. By focusing on what God has done for us, we can then give God the thanks he deserves.

You can also do this as a church. Just pass around a book and let every member have a few minutes to write down what he or she is grateful for. You can place this book where people can continually add to the list. This book of thanksgiving can serve as a constant reminder to the church of all the blessings that God has given.

Cultivate an attitude of gratitude

In 1 Thessalonians 5:16-18, Paul writes, "Be joyful always; pray continually; give thanks in all circumstances, for this is God's will for you in Christ Jesus." It is God's will that we give thanks in all circumstances. Regardless of the circumstances, we need to be grateful. Gratitude is an attitude. Gratitude is a condition of the heart.

We need to cultivate an attitude of gratitude. Some people are grateful by nature. Others of us have to work at it. God can give us a grateful heart. But we also need to do our part. We need to continually cultivate an attitude of gratitude. How can you do this?

- Spend time with people who have the "attitude of gratitude." Attitudes are contagious. Don and Donna Downer get everyone down. Find people who have a positive disposition. I guarantee you they are positive because they are grateful. Allow their attitude to influence your attitude.
- Begin each day with a short prayer of thanks. Start each day saying, "Thank you" to God. This will center your mind and help you to keep a grateful attitude throughout the day.
- Carry around your "Thanksgiving List" and every now and then get it out and take a look at it. Add something new to it. This will remind you to be grateful.
- Remember that gratitude is an attitude. When you find yourself getting negative, you've lost your attitude of gratitude. Stop for a moment and refocus. Count your blessings. Refocus your attitude of gratitude. It will help you through the day.

Dear God,

Cultivate in my heart an attitude of gratitude. Give me a grateful heart. Bring to my mind all the reasons I have to be grateful. If I forget to be grateful, stop me in my tracks and remind me of my blessings. Form in me the heart of Christ—a grateful heart.

Through Jesus
Amen

Endnotes

[1] Manning, *Ruthless Trust*, 24.
[2] Candace C. Moose, *The Grateful Heart: Diary of A Heart Transplant* (Cold Spring Harbor, New York: Rosalie Ink Publications, 2005).
[3] Ibid, 9.
[4] George Appleton, General Editor, *The Oxford Book of Prayer* (Oxford: Oxford University Press, 1985), 63.
[5] Source Unknown.

Chapter Nine
A Grace-filled Heart

Grace is something you can never get but only be given. There's no way to earn it or deserve it or bring it about any more than you can deserve the taste of raspberries and cream or earn good looks or bring about your own birth.[1]

–Frederick Buechner, spiritual writer

Amazing Grace
How sweet the sound
That saved a wretch like me
I once was lost
But now I'm found
Was blind but now I see.

'Twas grace that taught my heart to fear,
And grace my fears relieved;
How precious did that grace appear
The hour I first believed.

Through many danger, toils and snares,
I have already come;
'Tis grace has brought me safe thus far,
And grace will lead me home.

When we've been there ten thousand years,
Bright shining as the sun,
We've no less days to sing God's praise,
Than when we've first begun.[2]

–John Newton

My favorite contemporary Christian author is Philip Yancey. His writings move my soul. I love his book on Jesus entitled, *The Jesus I Never Knew*. I place it in the top ten of my favorite spiritual books. He has also written a book concerning grace. It is entitled, *What's So Amazing About Grace?* Nice title. In this book, Yancey defines grace. "Grace means there is nothing I can do to make God love me more, and nothing I can do to make God love me less."[3] He also writes:

> Grace makes its appearance in so many forms that I have trouble defining it. I am ready, though, to attempt something like a definition of grace in relation to God. *Grace means there is nothing we can do to make God love us more*—no amount of spiritual calisthenics and renunciations, no amount of knowledge gained from seminaries and divinity schools, no amount of crusading on behalf of righteous causes. *And grace means there is nothing we can do to make God love us less*—no amount of racism or pride or pornography or adultery or even murder. Grace means that God already loves us as much as an infinite God can possibly love.[4]

Perhaps you see why I like Yancey so much. He knows how to say things.

Grace. What does grace mean to you? The usual definition for grace is "unmerited favor." That's a fancy way of saying you're getting something for nothing. I like that thought.

I've also seen grace used as an acronym for God's riches at Christ's expense. Let's go with that definition of grace. GRACE=God's riches at Christ's expense.

God's Riches

> And my God will meet all your needs according to his glorious riches in Christ Jesus (Philippians 4:19).

> I pray also that the eyes of your heart may be enlightened in order that you may know the hope to which he has called you, the riches of his glorious inheritance in the saints (Ephesians 1: 18).

What does God have that we need? Just off the top of my head, I'd say, he has everything. Without God we would not be. And even when we are, when we leave God out of the picture, we cease to be. "In him we live and move and have our being" (Acts 17:28). That about says it all.

Without God, we are wretches—hopeless, hapless, helpless wretches. Without God, we are lost and blind. But God doesn't leave us lost and blind. He reaches down from his throne in heaven and picks us up from the pit and carries us to a new dimension of life—life to the full.

Have you ever seen a cat pick up one of her kittens? She opens her mouth and bites down on the back of the neck with enough pressure to pick her kitten up but with little enough pressure that it doesn't injure it. The kitten doesn't cry out in pain. The kitten surrenders to the jaws of its mother. This is a metaphor for God's grace. God reaches down from heaven and plucks us to safety by applying the right amount of pressure on us without forcing us to abandon our freewill.

Why does the mother cat do this for her kitten? I'm not willing to pick a kitten up in my mouth. She does this because the kitten is hers. As a parent, wouldn't you do anything for your child? When you have a newborn you feed her, clean her, burp her, change her, lose sleep for her, become an obsessive freak for her. Why? Because she is yours. God sees us as his. In spite of our sin, God sees us as his. And Jesus does the same. Helmut Thielicke noted:

> When Jesus loved a guilt-laden person and helped him, he saw in him an erring child of God. He saw in him a human being whom his Father loved and grieved over because he was going wrong. He saw him as God originally designed and meant him to be, and therefore he saw through the surface layer of grime and dirt to the real man underneath. Jesus did not *identify* the person with his sin, but rather saw in this sin something alien, something that really did not belong to him, something that merely chained and mastered him and from which he would free him and bring him back to his real self. Jesus was able to love men because he loved them right through the layer of mud.[5]

He loved us right through the layer of mud. That is grace. Jesus looked through our muck and loved us.

God is an unselfish God. He doesn't hoard his riches to himself. Whatever he has, he has in abundant supply, and he is willing to share out of his abundance with us. One commodity that has in abundant supply is grace.

I am deeply thankful for the grace of God. I need it every second of every minute of every hour of every day of every month of every year of every decade—you get the idea. Without it I am a wretch. I'm a mess with grace, but I am a big old slobberin' hunka, hunka burnin' mess without grace. That puts me in good company. That puts me in the company of the heroes of the faith who were all giant heaps of mess without grace. Remember Peter—he denied Jesus three times. Remember Paul—he persecuted the apprentices of Jesus. Remember James and John—super-competitive glory hogs. They needed grace. We need grace. I need grace.

When I think of grace, my biggest gawk of wonderment comes when I think about how often I mess up, but God's grace is always there. He continues to pull me from the pit time and time again. The disciple asked Jesus, "How often must we forgive? It is seven times?" Jesus answered, "No, not seven. Try seventy times seven." This is forgiveness *ad infinitum*. But in Jesus telling us how often we need to forgive, he is also reminding us of how often God has forgiven us. Jesus is always ready to forgive. God has abundant supplies of grace.

And I need grace. I mess up all the time. If I spent the next few pages cataloging my sins, you wouldn't want to read another word that I've written. You wouldn't want to ever hear from me again. But God wants to hear from me. Jesus wants to have fellowship with me. The Spirit still resides within me. That is grace. I don't deserve grace, but there it is. Heaping bowls of grace served up by God himself.

I love do-over's. What is a do-over? A do-over is when you are playing a video game and you die in the first couple of minutes, so you just start the game over. That's a do-over. A do-over is when you flunk an important test and the teacher takes your special circumstances under consideration and says, "Hey, Mr. Kinnard, you did terribly on this test, but out of the goodness of my heart, I'm going to let you retake it tomorrow." That's a do-over. And grace is God giving us a do-over. He looks down and says, "Hey, Steve you've really messed up your life, you've sinned against me, you deserve to die, but out of the goodness of my heart, I'm going to give you a second chance." Thank God for do-over's. Thank God for his abundant, amazing grace.

At Christ's Expense

> Why did my Jesus come to earth?
> And to the humble go?
> Why did he choose a lowly birth?
> Because he loved me so.
>
> Why did He drink the bitter cup
> Of sorrow, pain and woe?
> Why on the cross be lifted up?
> Because He loved me so!
>
> Till Jesus comes I'll sing His praise,
> And then to glory go,
> And reign with Him thro' endless days,
> Because He loved me so!
>
> He loved me so.
> He loved me so.
> He gave his precious life for me.
> Because he loved me so.[6]
> —James Daily

Consider these verses:

> You see, at just the right time, when we were still powerless, Christ died for the ungodly. Very rarely will anyone die for a righteous man, though for a good man someone might possibly dare to die. But God demonstrates his own love for us in this: While we were still sinners, Christ died for us (Romans 5:6-8).

> What, then, shall we say in response to this? If God is for us, who can be against us? He who did not spare his own Son, but gave him up for us all—how will he not also, along with him, graciously give us all things? (Romans 8:31-32).

These two passages are my two favorite passages about grace. They both express the tremendous love that God has for us. They also express the tremendous gift that God gave for our salvation. God loved us so much that he gave his own son to die on the cross for our sins. Grace is expensive. It costs God his son. It cost Jesus his life. Nothing compares.

What is the most expensive thing you've ever seen? I've seen the *Mona Lisa* at the Louvre in Paris. I waited in line while carrying my son on my shoulders in order to see it. It was smaller than I thought it would be. It was darker than I thought it would be. It wasn't quite so grand as I thought it would be. But it was worth the wait in line to see! It is priceless. I'll always have that memory.

I've seen the ceiling of the Sistine Chapel in Rome. I stood in line with my wife to see it. It was bigger than I thought it would be. It was brighter than I thought it would be. It was more than I thought it would be. It was definitely worth the time we stood in line and the price of admission to see it. I gawked in wonderment at it. I could have sat there staring up at that ceiling for days. I'll always have that memory.

Both the *Mona Lisa* and the ceiling of the Sistine Chapel are considered to be priceless. If they were destroyed, they could not be replaced. But I know something more valuable than the *Mona Lisa* and the paintings on the ceiling of the Sistine Chapel combined. It is one single human life. What is more priceless, more irreplaceable than a life? That is exactly what God and Jesus gave for us on the cross. Grace is expensive.

Grace cost Jesus his life. He came to the earth, took on flesh, lived among us and then died for our sins. That is grace. I don't understand it. I can only gawk at it.

Grace is amazing. Grace is expensive.

Receiving Grace

Like any other gift, the gift of grace can be yours only if you'll reach out and take it.
Maybe being able to reach out and take it is a gift too.[7]
—Frederick Buechner, spiritual writer

I love to give to charity, but I don't want to be charity.
This is why I have so much trouble with grace.[8]
—Donald Miller, spiritual writer

Grace is a free gift. And it is a very expensive free gift. It cost Jesus his life. But since it is a gift, it has to be received. If I were to send you an e-mail saying, "I have a free gift of unlimited grace just for you. Please respond!" How would you respond? There are five types of responses to God's grace:

The first type of response says, "Grace—what's grace?" These are people who don't receive God's grace because they don't acknowledge its existence. They just don't think about it. Grace doesn't even appear on their radar. They are so caught up in the here and now that they've given no thought to the hereafter. It's not so much that they reject grace, as much as, they don't even know it exists.

The second type of response says, "Grace? Thanks, but no thanks." These are people who know that grace is a good thing. They understand what it is about, but they don't want it in their lives. They feel okay as they are. They are self-sufficient. They believe in God, but they're doing just fine without his help. In a way, they turn up their noses at grace.

The third type of response says, "Thanks, but I'm not worthy." These are people who don't receive grace because they don't feel worthy of it. Donald Miller describes this reaction to grace:

> For a very long time, I could not understand why some people have no trouble accepting the grace of God while others experience immense difficulty. I counted myself as one of the ones who had trouble. I would hear about grace, read about grace, and even sing about grace, but accepting grace is an action I could not understand. It seemed wrong to me not to have to pay for my sin, not to feel guilty about it or kick myself around.[9]

When we think about what grace cost Jesus, we *should* feel hesitant about receiving it. But don't hesitate too long. Grace is not something to turn up your nose at. Recognize the great gift that God is offering you, and then gladly receive it.

The fourth type of response says, "Thanks for grace. I'll

start with a double portion and keep it coming, please." These are people who receive grace without realizing how precious grace is. They sidle up to grace like a hungry man sidling up to an all-you-can-eat lunch buffet. They love receiving grace, but they keep on sinning. Receiving grace doesn't motivate them to change. This cheapens the gift. Paul talks about this in Romans 6. He talks about some people who said, "the more we sin; the more grace we'll receive; so let's sin all the more and get grace all the more." Paul corrects them, "No! You're not thinking properly. Grace is expensive. Treat it with respect. When you receive grace, let it motivate you to stay out of sin." Which leads us to the fifth response.

The fifth type of response says, "Thank you for grace. I'll live a life worthy of this precious gift." These are people who understand the precious gift God offers in grace, and they receive the gift with gratitude and thanksgiving. After you've been around church a while, you can tell which people fall into this category. They are the ones who are incredibly thankful for their salvation. Their very lives are a thank-you letter to God. They are sincere. They are genuine. They are real apprentices of Jesus. They live each moment enveloped in God's amazing grace. They don't cheapen his gift. They value it. With their lives they sing, "Amazing Grace how sweet the sound; that saved a wretch like me. I once was lost, but now I'm found. Was blind, but now I see."[10]

Your Amazing Grace
A song. GSK. January 2001

Chorus:
Your Amazing Grace
Takes me to a place
Where I feel no disgrace
I wanna see your face
Your Amazing Grace
You make no mistakes
It keeps me in the race
To see you face to face
Your Amazing Grace

Verse One:
Life is like a spinning top
First I go and then I stop
Life goes up and life goes down
Life goes circles round and round

Then it messes with your mind
First see colors then you're blind
Wish I could jump this sinkin' boat
But I can't swim and I can't float

All the choices I have found
First seem certain then unsound
Tried to walk the razor's edge
But I plunged right off the ledge

First I'm strong and then I'm hurt
I'm a lovesick introvert
I'm so angry I could curse
Life's so shallow I could burst

So I look up to the sky
And I cringe and I scream and I question why?
I turn around, I find my place
When I see Your Amazing Grace

Verse Two:
Now I walk a different Road
And I carry a lighter load
Now I'm living upside-down
Once was lost but now I'm found

And I heed a higher call
He will catch me if I fall
He'll walk with me every day
On the straight and narrow Way

From the dark into the light
I will fight the noble fight
I once was blind but now I see
Once enslaved, but now I'm free

Now I look into the sky
And I cringe and I scream and I question why?
I turn around, I find my place
When I see Your Amazing Grace

⚜

Abba,

I cannot find the words to express to you the gratitude that I feel inside for your amazing grace. I know that without it I would be hopeless, hapless and helpless in a perishing world. You plucked me from the pit of darkness and transported into the brilliance of your kingdom of light. Thank you, thank you, thank you.

Help me to always have a grace-filled heart. Now and forever. Form in me the heart of your Son—a grace-filled heart.

In Him
Amen and Amen

Footnotes
[1] Frederick Buechner, 33.
[2] "Amazing Grace" was written by John Newton in 1779.
[3] Philip Yancey, *What's So Amazing About Grace?* (Grand Rapids: Zondervan, 1997), 71.
[4] Ibid, 70.
[5] Helmut Thielicke, *Christ and the Meaning of Life* (Grand Rapids: Baker Book House, 1975), 41.
[6] "Why Did My Savior Come to Earth?" Words and music by James Daily. Written in 1920.
[7] Buechner, 34.
[8] Donald Miller, *Blue Like Jazz* (Nashville: Thomas Nelson Publishers, 2003), 83.
[9] Ibid, 84.
[10] From the hymn "Amazing Grace" by John Newton.

Epilogue

Once there was a man who took a hike through a beautiful forest on a perfect spring day, a day when the weather was not too hot, nor too cold, but just right. The sun was shining brightly on that day. The sunshine broke through the tree branches and made shadowy forms on the forest floor. These shadowy forms looked like pixies dancing the dance of spring. The young man followed a path, which led to a fork in the road. The young man had a decision to make. He stood at the fork in the road and debated with himself which path to choose. The path to the left descended into the forest. It was clearly visible and well trodden. The path to the right was so overgrown with brush that it was almost invisible to the eye. It ascended at a relatively sharp angle. It was difficult to see, but what could be seen looked very dangerous.

Upon closer investigation, the man saw that the two roads were both marked with signs. The sign on the road to the left, the easy road, read, "The Way of Legalism." He had to dig out the sign on the road to the right, but once he had cleared it from the overgrowth, he found that it read, "The Way of the Heart." The young man was a novice hiker. But he had been learning the art of hiking from an older man who had been hiking all of his life. He remembered a statement that his mentor had said to him on an earlier hike, "Choose your path carefully. One of the greatest individual freedoms that you have in life is the ability to make your own choices. So choose your path wisely, because your path will determine your destination."

He sat down on his backpack, sipped some water from his canteen and reflected on his choices. He made his decision. He packed his canteen, threw his pack across his shoulders and turned to the right. He began to ascend sharply up the forest floor through thick underbrush and heavy shrubbery.

The journey was more difficult than he had anticipated. The slope of the path was steeper that he realized. He began to sweat. His muscles started to ache. His breathing became heavy. Each step was laborious. The undergrowth was so thick that it felt as if the shrubs were grabbing at his feet attempting to trip him. He began to wonder if he had picked the right road. He thought about turning back.

Then he remembered some special disciplines that his mentor had taught him in their walks together. His mentor taught him how to slow down his breathing, and this slowed down his heart rate. His mentor had taught him the importance of not getting ahead of himself, but to concentrate on every single step of the journey. His mentor had shown him the importance of enjoying the present moment no matter how strenuous or how difficult that moment might be. His mentor had taught him the importance of keeping his eyes focused down path to know where he was going. Be in the present, but don't forget the future. And his mentor had taught him that if things got too difficult, then just stop, sit, meditate, pray and search for guidance. These disciplines came in handy now. They helped him to trudge through the most difficult miles of the journey. The road seemed to be getting easier. But he actually wasn't certain if the road was getting easier, or if he was now more prepared for a difficult road.

He followed this path for a long while until it finally led out of the forest and into a meadow. It was a beautiful meadow with green grass and beautiful wild flowers that were swaying in the breeze. He stepped from the shadows of the forest into the sunshine of the meadow. His foot sank into the healthy grass. He laid down in the green meadow. He felt like he had no cares in the world. He felt free. He soon drifted into a peaceful sleep. After such a difficult journey, it was nice to rest. When he woke, he stretched his arms and legs and began to walk around the meadow.

He headed east. After walking about a hundred yards, he came upon some water. It was a crystal blue stream that cut its way along the eastern edge of the meadow. His mouth was parched. He bent down to drink from the stream, and he found the water quenched not just his physical thirst, but it seemed to quench a deeper thirst— a thirst deep in his soul.

He followed the stream south. He listened to the babbling brook as it led him along the edge of the forest to the southern part of the meadow. The brook sounded like music to him. He made up words and sang with the music.

After a few minutes, he stumbled onto a small vineyard. The vineyard was in perfect shape, and it was laden with fruit. He looked around for a caretaker, but he found no one. The vineyard seemed to take care of itself. He found a fruit on the vines that he had never seen before. It looked similar to grapes, but it was thicker and heavier than any grape he had ever seen. It was a yellowish orange color. Since he had never seen this type of fruit, he was uncertain if he should taste it or not. He knew that gardeners often marked their vines with signs that reminded them of the age of the vine and production of the vine from year to year. He poked around at the base of the vine until he found a small marker that read, "The fruit of the Spirit. Ever year is a good year. Help yourself to the fruit." He stood up and picked a fruit from the vine. It glistened in the sunshine.

He bit into the fruit and a taste gripped his taste buds like nothing he had ever tasted before. It seems to be that he was tasting life itself. With the first bite a feeling of love overtook him. With the second bite a sense of joy swept over his body. With the third bite he experienced a peace that went far beyond his understanding. With the fourth bite a wonderful sense of patience engulfed his soul. With the fifth bite he felt like he had been washed in pure goodness. With the sixth bite he felt a breeze of gentleness blow across his face. And with the seventh bite a feeling of self-control covered his entire being. Now he was full. But not full in his stomach. He was filled in his spirit. He felt mature, complete, satisfied. More satisfied in his soul that he had ever felt before.

He now reflected back on his journey. He thought back to his choice to follow the path marked, "The Way of the Heart." He was thankful that he had chosen the difficult path. He remembered how difficult it was in the beginning, but the direction of his mentor had helped him through the most difficult part of the journey. He reflected back on the words of his mentor, "Choose your path wisely, because your path will determine your destination." By choosing the way of the heart, he now enjoyed the fruit of the Spirit.

As the afternoon turned into evening, he again heard the brook playing her music in the background. This time the birds, the frogs, the crickets, and the katydids joined the symphony. He began to string together some words into a song:

Choose your path with great discretion
For it becomes your destination
Don't look for the easy way
For easy choices make you pay
Best to pick a difficult road
At the end, you'll lighten your load
This bit of wisdom I will impart
Always walk, "The Way of the Heart."

A prayer of St. Francis of Assisi

Lord, make me an instrument of your peace;
Where there is hatred, let me sow love;
Where there is injury, pardon
Where there is doubt, faith;
Where there is despair, hope;
Where there is darkness, light, and
Where there is sadness, joy.

O Divine Master,
Grant that I may not so much
Seek to be consoled as to console;
To be understood as to understand;
To be loved as to love;
For it is in giving that we receive;
It is in pardoning that we are pardoned;
And, it is in dying that we are born to eternal life.[1]

Abba Father,

Show us your way—the way of the heart. And keep us on your path.

In Jesus name
Amen

Endnotes

[1] Attributed to St. Francis of Assisi (1181-1226).

Bibliography

Appleton, George. General Editor. *The Oxford Book of Prayer*. Oxford: Oxford University Press, 1985.

Buechner, Frederick. *Wishful Thinking: A Theological ABC*. New York: Harper and Row, 1973.

_____. *The Hungering Dark*. San Francisco: Harper & Row, Publishers, 1969.

_____. *Listening to Your Life*. San Francisco: Harper San Francisco, 1992.

_____. *The Magnificent Defeat*. New York: The Seabury Press, 1979.

_____. *Now and Then*. San Francisco: Harper & Row, Publishers, 1983.

_____. *Peculiar Treasures: A Biblical Who's Who*. San Francisco: Harper & Row, Publishers, 1979.

_____. *A Room Called Remember: Uncollected Pieces*. San Francisco: Harper & Row, Publishers, 1984.

_____. *Son of Laughter*. San Francisco: Harper San Francisco, 1993.

_____. *Telling the Truth: The Gospel as Tragedy, Comedy, and Fairy Tale*. San Francisco: Harper & Row, Publishers, 1977.

_____. *Whistling in the Dark: An ABC Theologized*. San Francisco: Harper & Row, Publishers, 1988.

Carson, D. A. *The Expositor's Bible Commentary with The New International Version, Matthew*. 2 vols. Grand Rapids: Zondervan Publishing House, 1995.

Cloud, Henry and Townsend, John. *Boundaries*. Grand Rapids: Zondervan Publishing House, 1992.

_____. *How People Grow*. Grand Rapids: Zondervan Publishing House, 2001.

Crabb, Larry. *Inside Out*. Colorado Springs: NavPress, 1988.

_____. *The Pressure's Off*. Colorado Springs: WaterBrook Press, 2002.

_____. Shattered *Dreams: God's Unexpected Pathway to Joy*. Colorado Springs: WaterBrook Press, 2001.

Demarest, Bruce. *Satisfy Your Soul*. Colorado Springs: NavPress, 1999.

_____. *Soul Guide: Following Jesus as a Spiritual Director*. Colorado Springs: NavPress, 2003.

de Sales, Francis. *Introduction to the Devout Life*. New York: Image, 1972.

Eldredge, John. *The Journey of Desire*. Nashville, Tenn.: Thomas Nelson, 2000.

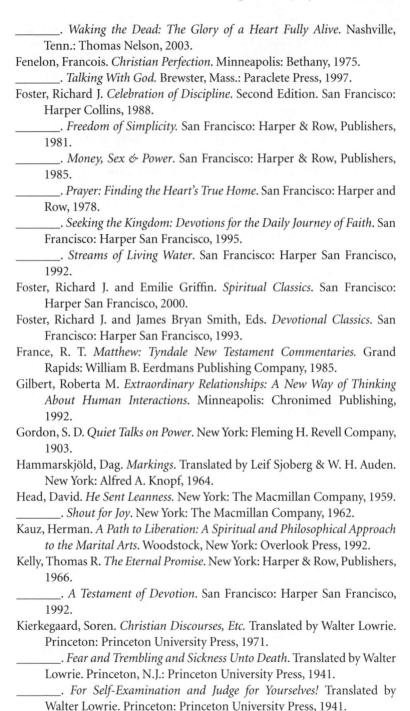

_____. *Waking the Dead: The Glory of a Heart Fully Alive.* Nashville, Tenn.: Thomas Nelson, 2003.

Fenelon, Francois. *Christian Perfection.* Minneapolis: Bethany, 1975.

_____. *Talking With God.* Brewster, Mass.: Paraclete Press, 1997.

Foster, Richard J. *Celebration of Discipline.* Second Edition. San Francisco: Harper Collins, 1988.

_____. *Freedom of Simplicity.* San Francisco: Harper & Row, Publishers, 1981.

_____. *Money, Sex & Power.* San Francisco: Harper & Row, Publishers, 1985.

_____. *Prayer: Finding the Heart's True Home.* San Francisco: Harper and Row, 1978.

_____. *Seeking the Kingdom: Devotions for the Daily Journey of Faith.* San Francisco: Harper San Francisco, 1995.

_____. *Streams of Living Water.* San Francisco: Harper San Francisco, 1992.

Foster, Richard J. and Emilie Griffin. *Spiritual Classics.* San Francisco: Harper San Francisco, 2000.

Foster, Richard J. and James Bryan Smith, Eds. *Devotional Classics.* San Francisco: Harper San Francisco, 1993.

France, R. T. *Matthew: Tyndale New Testament Commentaries.* Grand Rapids: William B. Eerdmans Publishing Company, 1985.

Gilbert, Roberta M. *Extraordinary Relationships: A New Way of Thinking About Human Interactions.* Minneapolis: Chronimed Publishing, 1992.

Gordon, S. D. *Quiet Talks on Power.* New York: Fleming H. Revell Company, 1903.

Hammarskjöld, Dag. *Markings.* Translated by Leif Sjoberg & W. H. Auden. New York: Alfred A. Knopf, 1964.

Head, David. *He Sent Leanness.* New York: The Macmillan Company, 1959.

_____. *Shout for Joy.* New York: The Macmillan Company, 1962.

Kauz, Herman. *A Path to Liberation: A Spiritual and Philosophical Approach to the Marital Arts.* Woodstock, New York: Overlook Press, 1992.

Kelly, Thomas R. *The Eternal Promise.* New York: Harper & Row, Publishers, 1966.

_____. *A Testament of Devotion.* San Francisco: Harper San Francisco, 1992.

Kierkegaard, Soren. *Christian Discourses, Etc.* Translated by Walter Lowrie. Princeton: Princeton University Press, 1971.

_____. *Fear and Trembling and Sickness Unto Death.* Translated by Walter Lowrie. Princeton, N.J.: Princeton University Press, 1941.

_____. *For Self-Examination and Judge for Yourselves!* Translated by Walter Lowrie. Princeton: Princeton University Press, 1941.

_____. *The Journals of Soren Kierkegaard:* A Selection Edited and Translated by Alexander Dru. London: Oxford University Press, 1938.

_____. *The Last Years: Journals 1853-1855.* Edited and Translated by Ronald Gregor Smith. New York: Harper & Row, Publishers, 1965.

_____. *Parables of Kierkegaard.* Edited by Thomas C. Oden. Princeton, N.J.: Princeton University Press, 1978.

_____. *The Prayers of Soren Kierkegaard.* Edited by Perry D. LeFevre. Chicago: University of Chicago Press, 1956.

_____. *Purity of Heart Is To Will One Thing.* Translated by Douglas V. Steere. New York: Harper and Brothers Publishers, 1938.

_____. *Training in Christianity.* Translated by Walter Lowrie. Princeton, N.J.: Princeton University Press, 1947.

_____. *Works of Love.* Translated by Howard and Edna Hong. New York, Harper & Row, Publishers, 1962.

Kinnard, G. Steve. *The Beginning of Wisdom.* New York: The New York City Church of Christ, 1988.

_____. *The Call of the Wise: An Introduction and Topical Index to the Book of Proverbs.* Waltham, Mass.: Discipleship Publications International, 1997.

_____. *The Crowning of the King: A Practical Exposition of the Gospel of Matthew.* Newton, Mass.: Illuminations Publishers International, 2004.

_____. *The Final Act: A Biblical Look at End-Time Prophecy.* Waltham, MA: Discipleship Publications International, 2000.

_____. *Getting the Most From the Bible.* Waltham, MA: Discipleship Publications International, 2000.

_____. *The Gospel of Mark: An Introduction to Discipleship.* Woburn, MA: Discipleship Publications International, 1995.

_____. *Holy Land Tour: The Gihon Spring.* (Video). New City, New York: G. Steve Kinnard, 2000.

_____. *Jerusalem: City of Promise.* (Video). New City, New York: G. Steve Kinnard, 1999.

_____. *New Wineskins: Formation of a Ministry of Multimedia Education Integrating the Bible, Geography and Archaeology.* New City, New York: G. Steve Kinnard, 1999.

_____. *Prophets: The Voices of Yahweh.* Waltham, Mass: Discipleship Publications International, 2001.

_____. Editor. *Undivided Devotion.* Waltham, Mass.: Discipleship Publications International, 1997.

_____. *The Way of the Heart.* Newton, Mass.: Illuminations Publishers International, 2006.

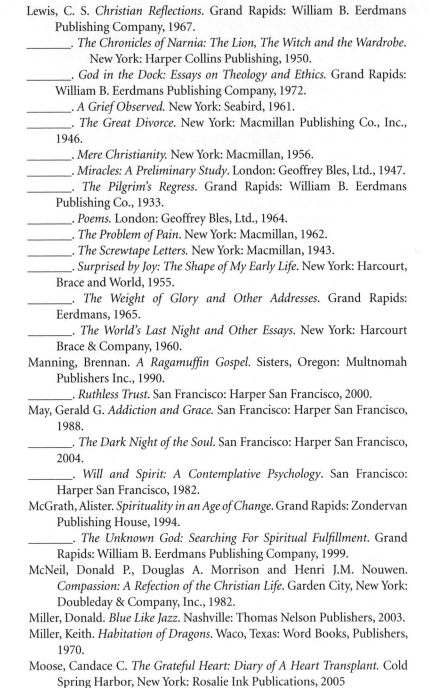

Lewis, C. S. *Christian Reflections*. Grand Rapids: William B. Eerdmans Publishing Company, 1967.

_____. *The Chronicles of Narnia: The Lion, The Witch and the Wardrobe*. New York: Harper Collins Publishing, 1950.

_____. *God in the Dock: Essays on Theology and Ethics*. Grand Rapids: William B. Eerdmans Publishing Company, 1972.

_____. *A Grief Observed*. New York: Seabird, 1961.

_____. *The Great Divorce*. New York: Macmillan Publishing Co., Inc., 1946.

_____. *Mere Christianity*. New York: Macmillan, 1956.

_____. *Miracles: A Preliminary Study*. London: Geoffrey Bles, Ltd., 1947.

_____. *The Pilgrim's Regress*. Grand Rapids: William B. Eerdmans Publishing Co., 1933.

_____. *Poems*. London: Geoffrey Bles, Ltd., 1964.

_____. *The Problem of Pain*. New York: Macmillan, 1962.

_____. *The Screwtape Letters*. New York: Macmillan, 1943.

_____. *Surprised by Joy: The Shape of My Early Life*. New York: Harcourt, Brace and World, 1955.

_____. *The Weight of Glory and Other Addresses*. Grand Rapids: Eerdmans, 1965.

_____. *The World's Last Night and Other Essays*. New York: Harcourt Brace & Company, 1960.

Manning, Brennan. *A Ragamuffin Gospel*. Sisters, Oregon: Multnomah Publishers Inc., 1990.

_____. *Ruthless Trust*. San Francisco: Harper San Francisco, 2000.

May, Gerald G. *Addiction and Grace*. San Francisco: Harper San Francisco, 1988.

_____. *The Dark Night of the Soul*. San Francisco: Harper San Francisco, 2004.

_____. *Will and Spirit: A Contemplative Psychology*. San Francisco: Harper San Francisco, 1982.

McGrath, Alister. *Spirituality in an Age of Change*. Grand Rapids: Zondervan Publishing House, 1994.

_____. *The Unknown God: Searching For Spiritual Fulfillment*. Grand Rapids: William B. Eerdmans Publishing Company, 1999.

McNeil, Donald P., Douglas A. Morrison and Henri J.M. Nouwen. *Compassion: A Refection of the Christian Life*. Garden City, New York: Doubleday & Company, Inc., 1982.

Miller, Donald. *Blue Like Jazz*. Nashville: Thomas Nelson Publishers, 2003.

Miller, Keith. *Habitation of Dragons*. Waco, Texas: Word Books, Publishers, 1970.

Moose, Candace C. *The Grateful Heart: Diary of A Heart Transplant*. Cold Spring Harbor, New York: Rosalie Ink Publications, 2005

Mulholland, M. Robert Jr. *Invitation to a Journey*. Downers Grove: InterVarsity, 1993.

_____. *Shaped by the Word: The Power of Scripture in Spiritual Formation*. Revised Edition. Nashville: Upper Room, 2000.

Neibuhr, Reinhold. *Leaves From the Notebook of a Tamed Cynic*. San Francisco: Harper & Row, Publishers, 1929.

Norris, Kathleen. *Amazing Grace: A Vocabulary of Faith*. New York: Riverhead Books, 1998.

Nouwen, Henri J. M. *Bread for the Journey*. San Francisco: Harper San Francisco, 1997.

_____. *A Cry For Mercy*. New York: Doubleday/Image, 1983.

_____. *Can You Drink the Cup?* Notre Dame, Ind.: Ave Maria Press, 1996.

_____. *Creative Ministry*. Garden City, New York: Doubleday and Company, Inc., 1971.

_____. *Here and Now*. New York: Crossroads, 1994.

_____. *In the Name of Jesus*. New York: Crossroads, 1992.

_____. *Life of the Beloved: Spiritual Living in a Secular World*. New York: Crossroad, 1992.

_____. *Making All Things New: An Invitation to Spiritual Life*. San Francisco: Harper & Row, 1981.

_____. *The Wounded Healer*. New York: Image Books, Doubleday, 1972.

Pirsig, Robert M. *Zen and the Art of Motorcycle Maintenance: An Inquiry Into Values*. Los Angeles: Audio Renaissance, 1974.

Powell, John. *Full Human Fully Alive: A New Life Through a New Vision*. Niles, Illinois: Argus Communications, 1976.

_____. *He Touched Me: My Pilgrimage of Prayer*. Niles, Illinois: Argus Communications, 1974.

_____. *The Secret of Staying in Love*. Niles, Illinois: Argus Communications, 1974.

_____. *Unconditional Love*. Niles, Illinois: Argus Communications, 1978.

Quoist, Michael. *The Breath of Love*. Translated by N.D. Smith. New York: Crossroads, 1987.

_____. *I've Met Jesus Christ*. Translated by J. F. Bernard. Garden City, New York: Doubleday & Company, 1973.

_____. *Prayers*. Translated by Agnes M. Forsyth and Anne Marie de Commaille. New York: Sheed and Ward, 1963.

_____. *With Open Heart*. Translated by Colette Copeland. New York: Crossroad, 1983.

Rauschenbush, Walter. *Christianity and the Social Crisis*. New York: Macmillan Company, 1912.

_____. *For God and the People: Prayers of the Social Awakening.* Boston: The Pilgrim Press, 1909.

_____. *A Gospel for the Social Awakening.* New York: Knickerbocker Press, 1950.

_____. *The Social Principles of Jesus.* New York: Association Press, 1919.

Richardson, Alan D., Editor. *A Theological Word Book of the Bible.* London: SCM Press, Ltd., 1957.

Rienecker, Fritz. Translated by Cleon L. Rogers, Jr. *A Linguistic Key to the Greek New Testament.* Grand Rapids: Zondervan Publishing House, 1976.

Sanders, J. Oswald. *Spiritual Leadership.* Chicago: Moody, 1967.

Scazzero, Peter with Warren Bird. *The Emotionally Healthy Church.* Grand Rapids: Zondervan Publishing House, 2003.

Schaeffer, Francis A. *The Church At the End of the 20th Century.* Downers Grove: InterVarsity Press, 1970.

_____. *The Church Before the Watching World.* Downers Grove: InterVarsity Press, 1971.

_____. *Escape From Reason.* Downers Grove: InterVarsity Press, 1968.

_____. *The God Who Is There.* Chicago: InterVarsity Press, 1968.

_____. *He Is There and He Is not Silent.* Wheaton, Ill.: Tyndale, 1972.

_____. *How Should We Then Live? The Rise and Decline of Western Thought and Culture.* Old Tappan, New Jersey: Fleming H. Revell Company, 1976.

_____. *The Mark of A Christian.* Downer Grove: InterVarsity Press, 1976.

_____. *True Spirituality.* Wheaton, Ill.: Tyndale, 1972.

Shaw, Scott. *The Warrior Is Silent.* Rochester, Vermont: Inner Traditions, 1998.

Smedes, Lewis B. *Forgive and Forget: Healing the Hurts We Don't Deserve.* San Francisco: Harper San Francisco, 1984.

Wardle, Terry. *The Transforming Path: A Christ-Centered Approach to Spiritual Formation.* Siloam Springs, Arkansas: Leafwood Publishers, 2003.

Welder, Laurence, Editor. *The Poets' Book of Psalms.* Edited by Laurence Wielder. San Francisco: Harper San Francisco, 1995.

Willard, Dallas. *The Divine Conspiracy.* San Francisco, Harper San Francisco: 1998.

_____. *Hearing God: Developing A Conversational Relationship With God.* Downers Grove: InterVarsity Press, 1984.

_____. *Renovation of the Heart.* San Francisco: Harper and Row, 1988.

_____. *The Spirit of the Disciplines.* San Francisco: Harper & Row, 1988.

"The With-God Life: The Dynamics of Scripture for Christian Spiritual Trans^ Formation: A RENOVARE International Conference on Spiritual Renewal," Conference Notebook. Englewood, Colorado: Renovare, 2005.

Woolman, John. *The Journal of John Woolman.* Boston: Houghton Mifflin Company, 1871.

Wright, N. T. *Colossians and Philemon,* Tyndale New Testament Commentaries. Grand Rapids: William B. Eerdmans Publishing Company, 1986.

Yancey, Philip. *Church: Why Bother?* Grand Rapids: Zondervan Publishing House, 1998.

_____. *Disappointment With God.* Grand Rapids: Zondervan Publishing House, 1988.

_____. *Finding God In Unexpected Places.* Nashville: Moorings, 1995.

_____. *The Jesus I Never Knew.* Grand Rapids: Zondervan Publishing House, 1995.

_____. *Rumors of Another World.* Grand Rapids: Zondervan Publishing House, 2003.

_____. *Soul Survivor: How My Faith Survived the Church.* New York: Doubleday, 2001.

_____. *What's So Amazing About Grace?* Grand Rapids: Zondervan Publishing House, 1997.

Journal Notes

Journal Notes

Journal Notes

Journal Notes

Journal Notes

Journal Notes

Journal Notes

Journal Notes

Journal Notes

Journal Notes

Journal Notes

Journal Notes

Journal Notes

Journal Notes

Journal Notes

Journal Notes

Journal Notes

Journal Notes

Journal Notes

Journal Notes

Journal Notes

Journal Notes

Journal Notes

Journal Notes

Journal Notes

Journal Notes

Journal Notes

Journal Notes

Journal Notes

Journal Notes

About Illumination Publishers International

Toney Mulhollan has been in Christian publishing for over 30 years. He has served as the Production Manager for Crossroads Publications, Discipleship Magazine/UpsideDown Magazine, Discipleship Publications International (DPI) and on the production teams of Campus Journal, Biblical Discipleship Quarterly, Bible Illustrator and others. He has served as production manager for several printing companies. Toney serves as the Managing Editor of Illumination Publishers International, and is the writer and publisher of the weekly "Behind the Music" stories and edits other weekly newsletters. Toney is happily married to the love of his life, Denise Leonard Mulhollan, M.D.

For the best in Christian writing and audio instruction, go to the Illumination Publishers website. Shipping is always free in the United States. We're commited to producing in-depth teaching that will inform, inspire and encourage Christians to a deeper and more committed walk with God.

www.ipibooks.com

ipi